Spaces of Creation

Spaces of Creation

The Creative Process of Playwriting

Suzan Zeder
with
Jim Hancock

HEINEMANN
Portsmouth, NH

Heinemann
A division of Reed Elsevier Inc.
361 Hanover Street
Portsmouth, NH 03801–3912
www.heinemann.com

Offices and agents throughout the world

The authors and publisher wish to thank those who have generously given permission to reprint borrowed material:

Reprinted with the permission of Simon & Schuster Adult Publishing Group from *Drawing on the Artist Within* by Betty Edwards. Copyright © 1987 by Betty Edwards.

"Labyrinth" by Mary E. Martin. Copyright © 2004 by Mary E. Martin. Reprinted by permission of the author.

Excerpts from *The Nature of Order: An Essay on the Art of Building and the Nature of the Universe (Book I: The Phenomenon of Life)* by Christopher Alexander. Copyright © 2002 by Christopher Alexander. Reprinted by permission from the Center for Environmental Structure, Berkeley, CA. All rights reserved.

Excerpts from *The Possible Human* by Jean Houston, copyright © 1982 by Jean Houston. Used by permission of Jeremy P. Tarcher, an imprint of Penguin Group (USA) Inc.

Library of Congress Cataloging-in-Publication Data
Zeder, Suzan.
    Spaces of creation : the creative process of playwriting / Suzan Zeder and Jim Hancock.
        p.   cm.
    Includes bibliographical references.
    ISBN 0-325-00684-9 (alk. paper)
    1. Playwriting. I. Hancock, Jim, 1931– II. Title.
    PN1661.Z43 2005
    808.2—dc22   2005012134

Editor: Lisa A. Barnett
Production editor: Sonja S. Chapman
Cover design: Catherine Hawkes, Cat & Mouse
Compositor: Valerie Levy / Drawing Board Studios
Manufacturing: Louise Richardson

Printed in the United States of America on acid-free paper
09 08 07 06 05 DA 1 2 3 4 5

To the creative artists
who have been our students and guides
on this journey.

CONTENTS

FOREWORD

by Naomi Iizuka

AS A PLAYWRIGHT AND A TEACHER OF PLAYWRITING, I SPEND A LOT OF time thinking about writing. Where do you start? *How* do you start? How do you mine your memories and dreams for ideas? How do you organize the raw material of life into a lucid and vibrant story? How do you endow characters flesh and muscle? How do you evoke an authentic sense of time and place? How do you coax a play into being?

In the spring of 2002, I came to the Michener Center at the University of Texas-Austin to teach playwriting. During that time, I had the good fortune of getting to know Suzan and Jim. They are both spectacular teachers. They bring a wisdom and passion to teaching that is truly remarkable. Over the years, Suzan and Jim have developed and refined an approach to the teaching of writing that is exciting and original. They have created a series of writing and movement exercises to get students to think in new ways about character, story, and structure. *Spaces of Creation* brings their decades of insights and wisdom together in one book.

Beyond teaching the craft of playwriting, *Spaces of Creation* teaches us about the far trickier and more ineffable question of creation. How do you find the story you want to tell? How do you find your own individual voice? Over the years, I've participated in many playwriting workshops as a student and then a teacher. I'm familiar with many different approaches to teaching writing. Suzan and Jim's approach is like nothing I have ever encountered before. Their insights into writing are absolutely original. Their exercises represent a radically innovative and tremendously effective approach to the writing process. Incorporating Suzan's decades of teaching playwriting and Jim's decades of teaching acting and movement, these exercises synthesize their insights into writing and movement in ways that are, I think, revolutionary. Whether you are a student or a teacher, whether you are writing within a university writing program or out in the world working on your own, whether you are just beginning or you've been writing for years, these exercises will guide you through the writing process in invaluable ways. They will help you write from your strongest and most authentic place. *Spaces of Creation* will crack open your writing process and make you a better writer.

There are some wonderful books about writing that are out there. They are illuminating and inspiring. I'm thinking, in particular, of books like Annie Dillard's *The Writing Life* or Jorge Luis Borges' *This Craft of Verse*. These are books I recommend to my students. Whether you're a playwright, a poet, or a fiction writer, these are books you should have in your library. These are books that you will read and reread. They will feed you for years to come. They will teach you more than simply craft. They will teach you how to become a better artist. *Spaces of Creation* falls into this select category. This is a book that every writer should have on their shelf. It is a book that you will return to over and over again through the years.

Spaces of Creation is a particularly important book for playwrights to read. Unfortunately, there seem to be an inordinate number of books about writing plays that approach the writing process in a bizarrely mechanistic way. In these books, writing a play becomes like building a car engine or baking a casserole. The premise of these books is that if you follow the diagram or the recipe, out will pop your finished play. The problem is that's not how you write a play. If you write plays, you know. Writing a play is not like putting together a particle board bookcase from Ikea. Writing a play is a lot more like walking through a jungle. Or deep-sea diving. Pick your metaphor. Writing requires that you traverse arduous and unknown landscapes. It requires that you coax skittish creatures out of their hiding places. It demands that you wrestle anacondas and stare down tigers.

Writing is a complex and unpredictable journey. It is a process in which you will draw upon your memories, your fears, and your dreams. It is a process that will engage all the muscles of your mind and body. It is a deeply personal process. The best teachers know this. Suzan and Jim are the best, and they know this well. In a beautifully lucid and engaging way, *Spaces of Creation* guides you through the writing process from that first moment of creation onwards. Breaking down the act of creation into a series of journeys through internal and external spaces, Suzan and Jim give you a host of exercises that will inspire and guide you. These exercises will help you mine your inner land-scape and your external world for ideas. They will help you find your voice. They will help you find the stories that only you can tell. They will help you bring those stories to fruition. *Spaces of Creation* will help you navigate the un-known terrain of the writing process. It is a wise book, the kind of book that will make you a better artist as well as a better writer. It will be a book you will read and reread for years to come.

ACKNOWLEDGMENTS

TO THE FOLLOWING INDIVIDUALS, FOR THEIR ASSISTANCE THROUGH THE long process of researching, writing, and living this book, we give our heartfelt thanks:

Rives Collins, who first glimpsed this creation and provided the space for it to grow

David Kranes, for helping us find the focus of space

Jane Barnette and Megan Gogerty, for millions of trips to the library

Sarah Myers, for meticulous proofreading and the gift of her insight

Donna Davis, for her drawings and the inspiration of her being

Karolyn Tybor, for "The Space of Fear" and help getting through it

Mary Martin, for her path through the labyrinth

The Graduate School of the University of Texas at Austin for the Faculty Research Assignment that allowed us time to finish this book

Labyrinth

I do not listen
for instruction
walking the labyrinth;
I lean into the curves
slowly spilling out
the unnecessary
accretions in life.

Walking your labyrinth,
rocks and crystals mark
the turnings in a valley
of your land, they cleanse
my path; their clear
and rough surfaces mirror
wisdom back to me
as I stop to fill
the center place
with a moment
of elation—of sky against
skin, of eyes against boundless
visions, how each of us is built
to accept all there is.

An igneous formation,
another shot of insight
caught and glorious
keeps me longer
before I spiral out,
leaning as I walk
now closer
to the rocks and crystals,
hear them ask me
to leave these words
as part of the labyrinth,
Of course I say yes, yes.

—Mary E. Martin

INTRODUCTION

THERE IS A LABYRINTH WHERE WE LIVE. IT IS FORTY-FIVE FEET ACROSS and contains more than seven hundred rocks and stones and chunks of ore and minerals and crystals, some weighing over one hundred pounds. Jim and I built the labyrinth together on the land of our Colorado writing retreat during the summer when forest fires raged within a few miles of our house. The forest service closed the national forest all around us and told us to listen for the blast on the sheriff's siren telling us to evacuate, but we did not leave. In the mornings, we cleared brush, cut trees, and swept up generations of pine needles as the air thickened with smoke and ash. In the afternoons, we built the labyrinth, stone by stone. In the evenings, we began writing this book. Each day the fire came closer, the smoke was denser, the danger was greater. We feared that we might lose the house, we might even lose the land, but the labyrinth would remain. Like a piece of writing that endures long after its creators are gone, the labyrinth promised the illusion of permanence.

I walked my first labyrinth six years earlier at the Playwriting Retreat at New Harmony in Indiana. I was there to work on a new play and Jim served as a movement resource for the company of actors and directors and writers. I arrived in New Harmony three days after finishing a seven-week course of radiation following a bout with breast cancer. I came to New Harmony desperate to find that place within myself that was still a writer. I found it in the labyrinth.

Each morni ng before writing and rehearsals, Jim and I walked the seven circles of the New Harmony labyrinth. Each day I found words waiting for me along the way; ideas unraveled, characters came, and step-by-step, I walked back into my writing self. At the center I found the creative person who had been lost in the turmoil of diagnosis, treatment, and recovery. So, it was entirely fitting that in another time of real and present danger, we would build a labyrinth of our own. The fire burned more than three thousand acres but spared our house and land. Living next door to the inferno taught us many things about working and being together in collaboration, about protecting what we love, about writing.

This book represents the culmination of twenty-five years of teaching playwriting and working with new plays for me, forty years of working with actors and teaching movement for Jim, and more than fifteen years of collaboration on what we have previously called Inner Sources for Out-Write Expression. This work originated in an intensive course we taught at a summer institute at Northwestern University organized by Rives Collins in 1989. At that time I had grown increasingly frustrated with the way I was teaching playwriting. I had based my own classes on familiar models in which students did writing exercises and brought scenes, acts, and whole plays to the table for discussion, resulting in a host of other people's opinions on what the playwright could have done or should have done to make the play "work." I was also concerned that many of the playwriting texts on the market seemed to be how-to manuals based upon Aristotelian models, which did not reflect the most current trends in writing for the theatre. In my experience, most classes, workshops, and books were curiously silent on the earliest phases of the process of creation, that delicate first stage of conception, when playwrights generate their initial ideas and form personal connections with their material. I had long felt that the most neglected writer's tool was the writer, but I didn't know how to put this awareness into practice. I had always admired Jim's work with actors on self-use and his ability to help his students find the fullness of their craft in the wholeness of themselves. For him, there seemed to be no separation of body and mind, and the breakthroughs made by his students resonated in their performances but also in their lives. When we were invited to teach that first Northwestern course, we began a path of discovery for ourselves and for our students that would lead us into new ways of combining the body and the mind in the process of writing.

We put together a highly eclectic, rather unorthodox mixture of disciplines and techniques, drawing from the fields of movement, visual art, anthropology, mythology, developmental and gestalt psychologies, dream analysis, and architecture. Over the years, the course at Northwestern expanded to include actors, directors, screenwriters, choreographers, poets, musicians, sculptors, ceramicists, business majors, teachers, and, of course, playwrights. The work was further developed in workshops, teaching residencies, seminars, and conference presentations all over the country. After every experience, participants clamored for us to write a book. Each time we said we would try.

Four years ago I began research for a course on the dramaturgy of space to investigate site-specific performance and to explore options other than traditional Aristotelian-based approaches to dramatic structure. I wanted to provide a context that might challenge my students to create fluid, imagistic, physical, and visually poetic plays and, at the same time, encourage them to look deep within themselves for their sources of inspiration. With the help of David Kranes, former artistic director of the Sundance Playwrights' Laboratory and professor of playwriting at the University of Utah, I began to focus on notions of space as the theoretical cornerstone of this inquiry. My reading took me on a circuitous path, from French philosopher Gaston Bachelard, to geographer Yi-Fu Tuan, to architect Christopher Alexander. The path wound round and round, but always at the center was this notion of the writer as a thinking, feeling, sensing, moving being with both body and mind. I began to see the creative process not as a sequential series of stages, but as space to be explored by the artist on a journey of discovery.

I realized that I had found the crystallizing concept and organizational framework for the book Jim and I had been trying to write! Within the generous galaxies of notions of space, it is possible to explore both the internal spaces of creation, where ideas and images and impulses are first perceived, and the external space of creation, where plays are written and produced. I found an ideological concept large enough to contain all that Jim and I had been trying to bring together about the creative process of writing and living a life in art.

In each of the following chapters, we invite you to explore a different kind of space. Within the inner landscapes of "Child Space," you will journey back to your own literal and metaphoric childhood to see what lessons the child who still resides within you has to teach about your writing and your life. In "Psychophysical Space," we delve into the connection between mind and body and discuss concepts of balance and the tensional forces that lead to movement and dramatic action. In "Interpersonal Space," we examine the physical and emotional territories and boundaries that exist between and among people and characters. In "Dimensional Space," we deal with the paradox of miniature and magnitude in the hopes of finding a sense of intimate immensity in multiple dimensions. "Sacred and Mythic Space" takes us back to archetypes and the stages of the hero's journey that serve as the foundation for ancient and contemporary quests and stories. "Dream Space" provides a path into the unconscious realms of imagery, symbolism, logic, and structure found on the other side of our eyelids whenever we go to sleep. In "Geographical Space," we look to the ways our sense of place affects theme, character, and language. In "Architectural Space," we find fascinating parallels between principles of architectural design and dramatic structure. Finally, in "The Space of Fear," we enter that territory that all of us know as artists but seldom speak about, the place where our fears and phobias dwell and prevent us from doing our best work.

One of the unique aspects of this book is its inclusion of activities and exercises drawn from various forms of movement training. Just as actors know that they must develop the resources of their minds and bodies, this book posits the notion that self-use principles drawn from movement are equally useful to writers to deepen their powers of perception, self-knowledge, and emotional availability. The writing exercises that accompany each chapter embrace techniques from visual art, music, and improvisation as a means of exploring character, theme, and plot in ways that do not always end in words.

Although the chapters in this book are arranged in a sequential order leading from internal notions of space (child and psychophysical space) to more external concepts (geographical and architectural space), this book has many points of entry. The essays encourage you to think widely about the subject of your art and the practice of your craft, while the exercises provide pathways to application in your own writing. In each chapter, Jim has provided an introduction to a different movement discipline related to a specific spatial concept. These exercises are designed to give you ease and economy of motion and to expand your awareness. The physical act of writing can be punishing, with hours spent sitting in a chair, staring at a keyboard. The movement exercises in this book can help you release tension and avoid chronic physical problems caused by negative patterns of habitual self-use.

Let your writing guide you through this book. If your play or performance piece deals with the domain of childhood, spend a bit of time in the playroom of "Child Space." If your plays dwell in the realm of dreams or use dream logic as a means of connecting events, slip into "Dream Space." If you are trying to evoke a specific physical location, you will find useful tools in "Geographical Space," and if structure is your concern, have a look at "Architectural Space" for some elegantly efficient models. The order is up to you!

Walking the labyrinth provides elegant metaphors for the process of writing and for your journey through this book. Your paths are circuitous but always lead back to the center, the self. The sojourn is active and involves both mind and body. The labyrinth is filled with discoveries; each is an entity unto itself but is also part of a larger whole. The individual stones of the labyrinth hold both past and future in a perpetual present tense. The path of the labyrinth always takes you out to the edges before delivering you to the center. What seems like a diversion is actually the shortest route. There are no wrong turns. Unlike a maze, the labyrinth is unicursal and requires only that you keep putting one foot in front of the other to lead you gently where you are going. It reveals, rather than instructs, and informs as you go. You walk it at your own pace, in your own time, for it is your journey, yours alone. In this book we hope that you will look within yourself to find what you hope to discover in your writing. We hope that you walk in confidence and joy!

Begin!

CHAPTER

Concepts of Space and Processes of Creation

CONCEPTS OF SPACE

THE IDEA OF SPACE IS A SLIPPERY CONCEPT, NOTORIOUSLY HARD TO contain in a single definition, and yet the notion of space is at the absolute heart of everything we do in life and in the theatre. Playwrights create space by weaving words and actions, images and ideas into imaginary worlds. Designers build these worlds in three dimensions with the physical elements of sets, costumes, light, and sound. Directors shape space, bringing worlds to life with staging and modulating the dynamics of performance. Actors and dancers inhabit space physically and emotionally as they create characters and execute choreography. Audiences come together with performers in real time and actual space to turn a play into a performance. But for each of these creators there is also a different kind of space: the internal space of mind and body where he or she first formed the idea of what an imaginary world could be, what it might mean, and how it might be made. It is this internal space of creation, and how it feeds and fuels the playwright's process, that concerns us in this book.

The quandary of how space affects the way we make meaning in our lives and in our art has fascinated physicists, psychologists, philosophers, poets, and painters as well as playwrights. It is useful for us, as makers of theatre, to find ways of thinking and talking about space in the widest possible context, before narrowing the scope of our concern to our own plays and processes of creation. In the chapters that follow, we will explore the spaces of our childhoods, our minds and bodies, our sacred beliefs and myths, our dreams, and our fears in the hopes that these journeys will lead us to new places in our work as writers. At the beginning of this adventure, however, we start with that most familiar and universal of all spaces, the house.

In his seminal work, *The Poetics of Space*, French philosopher Gaston Bachelard discusses the meanings of domestic and natural space as means of exploring what he calls the "poetic image." Using space as his lens, he shows us how our perceptions of houses, nests, shells, and other shelters shape our thoughts, memories, and dreams. The notion of house as both a physical space and a metaphysical concept furnishes us with a body of images that serve as metaphors for our psychological and social selves. The deeper connotations of seemingly simple dwelling spaces provide us with poetic images that help crystallize concepts of ourselves in society.[1] In the consolation of caves, humans and mammals gather in groups for mutual comfort and support. But in the solitude of shells, creatures dwell singly in shelters that protect and isolate them. We often speak of nesting to mean nurturing. Bachelard offers the example of a bird's nest, which offers a primal image of caretaking. The mother bird uses her own body to form the shape of the nest. After she gathers twigs and branches and bits of grass, she then turns her body round and round until the nest conforms to the shape of her own breast. With elegant economy, she is both architect and occupant of a dwelling made for the sole purpose of caring for her young. Her house is quite literally built from her own body, and this image resonates with us as a metaphor on a deeply human level.

Just for a moment, consider the spaces you move through every day and how they shape and determine your experience. Your workspace, whether it is an office or an open field, accommodates or inhibits the work you do. How is your attitude about your work affected by the space in which it takes place? Consider your home space. How is it different from your workspace? How does it reflect your personality? How does it accommodate your needs? Does it shelter and protect you, or does it isolate and inhibit you? Is it a cave, a nest, or a shell? Think about the space where you do your creative work. How does it inhibit or release your thoughts? How does it hold your body? How does your space define you? How do you define your space?

In *Man and His Symbols*, psychologist Carl Jung presents the house as a symbol of the unconscious, which indicates the multiple layers of the human psyche. To dream of a house is to glimpse the dimensions of the self in all of the levels and layers of its complexity.[2] To both psychologist and philosopher, the house is a very powerful metaphor.

What are the dwellings of your dreams? Do you return to the houses of your childhood or do you travel to fantastical palaces possible only in your imagination? Is there a pattern or recurring theme in the kinds of houses your mind visits in sleep? What messages do these images suggest to you? Do these dwellings ever appear in your writing?

Space and Place

The notion of place is similar to that of space, yet place tends to be more lo-calized and concrete than space. According to theories of human geography, place is bounded space, a portion of space occupied by a person or a thing. Place is given meaning and significance by the attachments and memories we associate with a specific location, object, artifact, or event. The memory of a bedroom from our childhood is held in a host of sensory impressions: the color of the wallpaper, the feeling of the rug where we played with our toys, the slant of light through the window, the smell of crisp sheets. We remember this place with all of our senses. We carry the vast recesses of child space in our minds, muscles, and memory.

The same is true for geographic space. We each come from a particular country, region, state, city, and neighborhood, but these locations are gener-alized until they are made manifest in our personal rhythms, speech patterns, attitudes, and memories, which tie us to and identify us with a particular place. Space is general; place is specific. Space is fluid and flexible, but place is fixed and filled with feelings. Space is universal, but place is our own. Place is time and space made visible.

Objects can hold similar associations and attachments for us when we im-bue them with special significance; in this, they function like place. Everyday objects take on enormous significance as we give them meaning through our experience. The power of all the arts, and playwriting in particular, is to trans-form space into place and to create an emotional connection with such clarity that an audience feels what the characters feel. When the Gentleman Caller breaks Laura's unicorn in *The Glass Menagerie*, he breaks her heart and our own.

Loss is what we feel when we lose the bearings that orient us to place and are cast adrift into space, undifferentiated and unknown. Our sense of spatial organization allows us to feel safe in our surroundings. This comfort allows us to pass through the environment without really paying too much attention to it. We concentrate on where we are going as opposed to where we are, but when we lose that connection to destination, we feel lost and the space around us seems to change. If we are walking in a forest, the path seems rougher, the trees are suddenly huge and forbidding, even the sounds are more intense. In fact, the forest is exactly the same as before we were lost, but our perception is entirely different. Suddenly, the familiar becomes unfamiliar.

In his essay "Art as Technique," Russian formalist critic Victor Shklovsky speaks of "defamiliarization" as one of the chief objectives of a work of art. The artist's ability to take a familiar theme, image, idea, or emotion and make it unfamiliar allows an audience to fully experience its power.[3] Stephen Sondheim's musical journey *Into the Woods* provides a very different perspective on familiar fairy-tale characters we know all too well. This difference allows us to experience their stories in a new way.

The feelings of defamiliarization and loss associated with grief are also spatially related. When we lose people who are dear to us, our emotional moorings are cut away and we are cast adrift in our own lives without the anchors they provided. It is a paradox that those we have lost are often more present in their absence than before they were gone. We are haunted by the presence of their absence. Loss is one of the primary themes in all of art but particularly in theatre. Think back on the plays that have truly touched your life and moved you emotionally. Chances are that themes of loss and longing lay at the center of these pieces, not in a cheap exploitation of sentimentality, but in a way that allowed you to feel these emotions as if for the first time and to experience them as your own. To recognize the reflection of yourself in another is a form of empathy.

One of the primary functions of art is to create place out of space in a journey of discovery through unfamiliar territory, where even if the terrain is known, it is experienced anew. This may be an outward expedition where specific geographical locations are suggested in sensory impressions captured in the playwright's craft. In the dialogue of David Mamet, we hear the rhythms and tempos of urban Chicago; through the characters of Horton Foote, we come to know rural Texas; the early plays of Beth Henley transport us to small-town Mississippi; and the themes of Samuel Beckett take us to the heart of nowhere. As the artist travels, so does the audience. The purpose of this book is to provide paths of access for both.

Space and Performance

Notions of space are fundamental to all artistic pursuits. Visual artists use the relationship between positive and negative space and principles of composition in paintings, drawings, photography, and sculpture. In music, the spatial arrangement of notes controls rhythm, harmony, melody, and tempo. Choreographers use time, space, and weight to create patterns with bodies in motion. Playwrights are concerned with the internal space where the idea for the play is born, the physical space of the world of the play, the interpersonal space that exists between characters, the pace and velocity of events, and, finally, the theatrical space that determines the relationship between spectators and performers.

In *Space in Performance*, Gay McAuley points out that theatre is, perhaps, unique among the arts in that the name of the discipline is the same as the name of the physical location where it often takes place. Theatre is both a place and an art form.[4] But the performance of theatre does not always take place in a physical space specifically designed for that purpose. The essence of theatre is what happens between a performer and a spectator. Although a live performance may be repeated, it will never have exactly the same dynamics more than once. Each audience brings its own particular energy that is as much a part of the event as the production.

In our post-postmodern era there is a lively semantic debate between the semiotics of theatre and performance. Although we may quibble about terminology, the fact of the matter is that live performance will always have a spatial component because it has to happen somewhere and is always embodied in the physical bodies of the performers and spectators. Although space has always had a profound effect upon both the form and the content of performance, now, perhaps more than ever before in theatrical history, our definitions have widened and expanded to include an astonishing variety of performance forms and practices. The influences of visual arts, installations, and interdisciplinary artists, such as Anna Halprin, Meredith Monk, and Deborah Hay, have brought the multiple languages of dance and movement and the visual forms of photography, video, and film into the performance arena. A host of bright, articulate, experimental playwrights, including Erik Ehn, Mac Wellman, Suzan-Lori Parks, and Ruth Margraff, has redefined our concepts of theatrical language and poetic diction. Cross-disciplinary artists such as Lisa D'Amour and Daniel Alexander Jones have broadened the conversation and blurred the distinction between performance ethnography and playwriting. Collaborative creations by companies such as Blue Man Group and Rude Mechanicals have challenged the notion of playwright-director-actor hierarchies.

Building on the environmental theatre movement of the 1960s and '70s, contemporary playwrights and directors create site-specific productions in which nontheatrical spaces function as primary elements in the dramatic structure of the performance. Political outrage and social activism have fueled the theories and practices of Augusto Boal and his many followers. Boal's concept of Invisible Theatre erases any distinction between performance and spectator space to such an extent that the "audience" is often unaware that a theatrical event is even taking place. All of these diverse forms of theatrical practice have one thing in common: they happen in real time and in a physical space shared with an audience.

With so much abundance, it is hard to find a vocabulary with which to discuss the process of creation of so many diverse forms. In my work with students, playwrights, and performance artists, I have found it useful to enter into this conversation through an exploration of the kinds of spaces they might inhabit in mind and body as they create their theatrical worlds and see them come to life in performance.

PROCESSES OF CREATION

The process of creation is different for every person who attempts to solve a particular problem in an original way or to express an idea, feeling, or concept through an artistic medium. In most cases the work begins in isolation following the glimmer of an impulse, image, idea, memory, character, or concern. Sometimes other source material serves as a stimulus: a myth, legend, or fable, a historical event, a true story, an item from the newspaper, a provocative issue or an injustice. The process of creation may also be a group venture, with all phases of perception, conception, and execution of a project undertaken by a collective, ensemble, or devising team in which creators come together, united by a shared question or concern. This common ground becomes the space of collaboration.

Theories of creativity and creative process are as diverse and slippery as those of space. From scholarly studies to slick self-help books, educators, psychologists, educational theorists, and self-styled gurus have struggled to find ways to define, identify, measure, develop, promote, package, and market creativity. Research on the conundrum of creativity abounds in a variety of scientific and educational contexts as well. Educational theorists, such as Howard Gardner and Vera John-Steiner, look to the individual and social conditions that have contributed to the creative output of famous figures in the arts and sciences.

In his book *Creating Minds*, Gardner stresses the importance of childhood influences and the ability of the "creator" to maintain a childlike curiosity and capacity for wonder even into adulthood. Einstein was able to return to the conceptual world of childhood in his search for understanding, unhampered by the limitations of conventional scientific thought. The puzzles and questions of his youth later fueled his most important discoveries.[5] In *Creative Collaboration*, John-Steiner contends that creative activities are social interactions and stresses the importance of collaborators, even with innovations thought to be solo creations. For example, composer Igor Stravinsky's interaction with choreographer George Balanchine helped define and develop Stravinsky's musical innovations.[6]

Both Gardner and John-Steiner focus their attention on accomplished and recognized artists, scientists, historians, and political figures. But what of the everyday creator: the painter, poet, playwright, musician, mathematician, or inventor living outside the rarified glare of public scrutiny and approval? What of the quilter who takes scraps and pieces of fabric and turns them into masterpieces of intricacy and design but stubbornly insists, "I'm not creative!"? In both of her popular books on drawing, *Drawing on the Right Side of the Brain* and *Drawing on the Artist Within*, arts educator Betty Edwards articulates a humane and down-to-earth approach to examining the creativity that dwells within all of us and not just a select few.

Seeing and Knowing

The relationship between seeing and knowing is crucial to an understanding of creative activity. Edwards points out that much of our vocabulary relating to concepts of knowing and understanding is expressed in visual terms. When we understand something, we often exclaim, "Oh, I see," when what we mean is "Oh, I understand." Many of our concepts of creativity are also expressed in visual metaphors. Creativity is the ability to "see things in a new light."[7]

It is commonly believed that creative activity involves both the right and the left brain hemispheres, the two major modes of brain functioning that make up human thought. These contrasting but complementary systems for processing information are closely related but fundamentally different. Left-brain thinking tends to be linear, logical, and language-based whereas right-brain functioning tends to be more visual, spatial, and nonverbal. The right brain grasps overall concepts and finds relationships between pieces of information while the left brain is concerned with symbols, literal meanings, and measurements. The right brain is spontaneous, intuitive, and playful while the left brain is sequential and analytical. On the surface it might seem that the right brain is the more creative of the two, but both modes of brain functioning are necessary for creative thought.

Stages of Creative Process

In *Drawing on the Artist Within*, Edwards synthesizes theoretical speculations on the stages of creative process into five discrete but interrelated phases: *insight, saturation, incubation, illumination,* and *verification*. These five stages can be applied to any endeavor that requires a creative solution, from trying to move a heavy rock out of a deep hole to finding the name of a character in a play. When I was trying to find the name of the protagonist for my play *Mother Hicks*, I experienced all five stages of this process over a period of months. Last summer when Jim was building the labyrinth, he experienced the same sequence in a matter of hours as he struggled with some heavy lifting of his own. My students find these stages to be relevant to their work as playwrights, as they recognize similarities to their own unarticulated processes as part of a larger whole.

The first stage is that of insight. This is the first spark of inspiration, the initial imaginative leap that leads to the formulation of the problem to be solved. In that first instant, an image or notion of the finished whole is sensed by the right brain as an impression but is not yet known on a conscious level. In the case of the heavy rock, Jim saw that it was in a deep hole, but he imagined it in the labyrinth in just the perfect spot. As for the character in my play, she came to me as a total presence in voice, body, feelings, and fears. I knew everything about her except her name.

The second phase is saturation, or information gathering. It consists of a search for relevant pieces of information that might fit with the notion of the whole, glimpsed in the previous stage. This is primarily a left-brain activity that tends to be a lengthier process than the first spark of insight. Various solutions are considered and tried on for size. For the rock, Jim tried to make the hole larger, he tried a wedge, he even asked me to help lift, but it was still too heavy. As for the missing name, I checked the telephone directory and went to the library for "what to name the baby" books; I even found an old graveyard and searched for possibilities on tombstones.

The third phase, incubation, is so closely related to saturation that they seem to take place simultaneously. Incubation is what the mind does with the information gathered during saturation. The right brain tries to find the overall pattern to the information provided by the left brain. For the rock, Jim said, "Try lifting, try pulling, try hauling, try a jackhammer! "Who's got a jackhammer?" The constant back and forth between saturation and incubation creates an emotional friction, a creative tension that often feels like anxiety but is, in actuality, just a good and healthy part of the process. This is often the most difficult time for the writer. It can feel like a block, like *no* activity is taking place. Actually, a great deal of activity is going on; as with a humming-bird that appears to hover in mid-air, the wings of your imagination are moving too fast to be seen. Frustration builds and produces cognitive dissonance, but this is not necessarily a destructive force. Entropy, or a lack of creative tension, is what you have to fear because it can lead to the despair and self-doubt that can shut the process down. Creative tension, on the other hand, is often uncomfortable, but it propels the work forward!

The fourth phase, illumination, literally comes in a flash. Creative tension builds to a point where it cannot go any further, and—*pow*—something shifts in awareness; the solution comes in an instant as a knowable thing. The right brain presents the answer and the left brain recognizes it. The release of tension is a joyful explosion of energy; the light comes on. Jim rigged up a lever and popped that rock out of the hole! One rainy morning while I was walking my dog, I suddenly realized that my character didn't have a name because no one had ever named her.

The fifth and final stage is verification. The solution is acted upon. The rock went flying out of the hole and Jim rolled it into the labyrinth. As for my character, the young protagonist known simply as Girl began searching for the name that had eluded me. Verification, like saturation, may take a very long or very short time, depending upon the nature of the creative problem to be solved. It may be a matter of writing a single line, making a crucial decision, crafting a scene, or writing the whole play, but verification is only the act of recording the result of all the stages that have gone before. All too often we think of this stage as the entire process. We mistakenly believe that only the time spent at the keyboard or in production really matters, when in truth, all parts of the process are equally vital. There is a well-known story about a famous painter who was simply sitting by a roadside on a summer afternoon when an acquaintance asked why he wasn't painting.

"Oh, but I am!" he replied. When the friend objected, saying he saw no canvas or brushes or paint, the painter pointed to his forehead and said, "Here, I am painting!"

For writers it is good to remember that the time spent staring out a window or facing a blank page is as much a part of the process as the time spent typing. Quiet time walking your dog or working out in the gym can also be writing time. A playwright's moment of illumination might, and probably will, come when it is least expected and most needed. To think of the finished scene as simply a verification of what you discovered in the previous four stages somehow takes the pressure off the need for perfection and keeps the process fluid, flexible, and always evolving.

The description of these five stages sounds deceptively simple, and it is easy to forget that the act of creation can be exhausting. It takes enormous physical, mental, and emotional energy to work through all of the five stages from insight to verification and then to do it again and again. The creative tension caused by the friction of saturation and incubation wears out your body as it numbs your mind. It's a long, hard climb up the hill to the moment of illumination, and the spiral down into verification can be filled with doubt and despair. Sometimes, sitting in a chair and staring at words on a page for six or seven hours at a stretch can be the hardest work you'll ever do. By comparison, lifting rocks is easy. The act of creation is backbreaking, soul-searing work. Even God had to rest after just six days.

SPACE AND CREATION

In this book, Jim and I hope to present an alternative approach to the process of playwriting that might also be applied to other forms of creative activity and inquiry. If we view our creative work as a labor, as something we *do*, the Sisyphean toil of constantly pushing the rock uphill, we are focusing on the effort required. It is easy to become discouraged. But if we look at process in spatial terms, and think of creativity as space we explore and space we create for others to explore, then perhaps we'll find a path that leads to the joy of discovery. Each space of creation has its own topography, its own laws of physics and a geography unique unto itself. In the first phase of insight, we glimpse where we are going, but no amount of planning or speculation can tell us what is there until we go there physically, mentally, and emotionally. We are a bit like the early cartographers who mapped mountains as they climbed them. They let the land tell them how the map must be drawn.

The space of creation exists within each of us in our brains and our bodies. It is where we formulate our ideas, where all our past experiences and feelings are filed away in the memory of mind and muscle. Below the surface of our waking world are unconscious territories where we have hidden what we do not wish to remember, where fears and phobias, too powerful to name, appear as shadows. These are rich and fertile landscapes for us to explore in our work as writers, but access to these deeper dimensions of self is sometimes difficult. This space is sometimes so private that we deny access of ourselves to ourselves. We may be unaware that there is a deeper level, or we may be content to rest on the surface of our thought, feeling, and experience. Lots of writers make their livings writing what has been written before and are paid good money to do so, churning out screenplays, television scripts, scenarios, and even plays based on familiar models and tropes. But this is rarely the writing that changes the field or the artist. To do that, you must go deeper into territory that is uncharted and new.

The following chapters will present a series of spatial metaphors for you to explore in yourselves and in your work. Each will begin with a discussion of a different space from a variety of perspectives (physical, philosophical, psychological, etc.), followed by practical exercises and activities to help you relate these concepts to your own self-discovery or to apply them to the plays you are writing. The inclusion of physical work through a variety of movement disciplines is absolutely essential. Access to your own creative space is often most effective when first experienced through the body and then through the mind. This helps us avoid the obvious trap of overintellectualizing. It also acknowledges the fact that mind and body are one and that even the writer who never leaves his or her chair is still engaging in arduous physical activity.

We encourage you to enter these spaces with an open mind and heart. Only by exploring them with all your senses will you know how these experiences might be valuable to you in your own work. If you wish to discover a new space within yourself and within your work, you have to be willing to toss aside the map of where you have been. You have to be willing to get lost. Only then will you be able to go somewhere you have never been before.

MOVEMENT: WARM-UP FOR WRITERS

The body and mind are inextricably connected, but many writers tend to depend on the mind and ignore the body as they sit for hours at a time, staring at a page or computer screen, thinking that they are exercising only their fingers. All of us are psychophysical beings. Physical activity is a reflection of your emotional life. Your muscular system is controlled by your brain. The challenge becomes one of maintaining balance and logic between inner impulse and outward expression, be it written or verbal. The goal of the physical work that you will find described in this book is to provide greater access to your own inner resources for expression through improved self-use, more ease and economy of motion, and less stress.

A writer sits in one place for long periods of time. Depending on how one sits, stress and fatigue will occur before long, and this can begin to affect the mind. One doesn't think as clearly, ideas don't flow, the translation of thought to the page is inhibited, and frustration sets in. A restricted, tightly bound, tense body does not allow for keen perception, expansive ideas, and the confidence necessary for creative work.

Over many years of teaching and working with both writers and actors, we have discovered that unlocking the body through a variety of physical disciplines can have a profound effect upon unlocking the mind. Most of my writing classes begin with or include some physical work. Most of Jim's movement classes involve some form of writing. Our approach has been emphatically eclectic, drawing on a variety of systems and techniques, including the work of F. M. Alexander, Moshe Feldenkrais, Michael Nebadon, and Bonnie Bainbridge Cohen. The work of each of these people will be discussed in greater detail in the following chapters.

Warm-Up Exercises
All of these exercises can be done while sitting at a desk and without stopping your thought process or writing.

Breath
First, the breath. There are many approaches to breath awareness. Breathing is a natural process. We don't need to be taught how to breathe, but rather, to be shown how to accommodate breath. Shallow breathing is the norm but is not best for a healthy physical response. Mouth breathing is the norm but not as beneficial as nose breathing. Upper-chest breathing is the norm as opposed to a more dynamic full-body breath. Breath becomes full-bodied when inhalation is done through the nose, resulting in a fuller lung capacity and more total muscular response. The awareness of filling in the back is helpful for full breaths because of the anatomical fact that the lungs are located closer to the back than to the front of the body.

The Alexander Technique has a breath approach called the whispered "Ah."

Take breath in through the nose, and then release it by allowing the jaw to release and the lips to lightly open.

The tongue will rest in the bottom of the mouth, with the tongue tip resting behind the lower front teeth.

It is the sound of the breath, not vocalizing the release of breath, that allows it to be natural and not forced out.

It is helpful, upon releasing the breath, to think of allowing the spine to release upward.

Practice the whispered "Ah" for respiratory control and to stimulate vital mental and physical energy.

Face

The next exercise has three steps, all of which are important to being present and consciously allowing yourself to discover a greater awareness.

Think a smile.

> This direction of thought will tend to raise the soft palate, which allows for a larger oral cavity and will release the jaw (a major place of tension in the body). You do not have to literally smile, but *think it*.

Brighten the face.

> This direction is not intended to force a startled look on your face, but it activates the facial muscles and tones them. It releases the forehead (another place in the body where we hold tension, often unconsciously and habitually), the jaw, and the eyes.

Release the eyes.

> This direction of thought allows for greater peripheral vision and softens the eyes, which, in turn, releases the neck and encourages easier breathing. The eyes are released out to the sides as you focus, instead of the more common narrowing of focus.

Pelvis

A tight jaw reflects tension and can often be traced to a held or rigid pelvis. An improperly aligned pelvis can result in lower back problems.

Assume that you are sitting on a clock face with twelve o'clock toward your head.

Tilt the pelvis (and *not* the torso) down toward six o'clock. Notice how this restricts breathing, tightens the chest, and deepens the lumbar, which affects alignment.

Now, tilt the pelvis up toward twelve o'clock. Notice how this collapses and restricts the viscera, adding compression to the body.

Tilt the pelvis toward nine o'clock (this will require lightly lifting one hip upward). Be aware of how familiar this might feel, which often indicates that you sit with your weight inefficiently shifted to one side. This causes a muscular imbalance and restriction, which can shorten one side of the body, thus throwing your alignment out of balance.

Tilt the pelvis toward three o'clock. Be aware of which side feels more familiar or comfortable. Remember that comfort may be familiarity, not balance.

After exploring all of the above, rotate the pelvis while specifically touching all those clock numbers.

Rotate in one direction, and then reverse the direction.

Legs, Feet, and Pelvis

Since sitting is a static position and the way in which you sit is important, it behooves you to not cross the legs or tuck them too far under your chair. Although one of these positions may seen more comfortable, consider it to be familiar and habitual and not necessarily *correct* for ease and a physically balanced relationship. Your nerve endings are in the feet and hands, and it is important that you attend to those areas. The feet tend to be more neglected than the hands in that respect.

Starting with the right leg, in a seated position, lift the heel; slide the foot forward into a full extension while on the ball of the foot.

Keeping the heel lifted, slide the foot back to its original position.

Repeat several times.

Drop the knee outward to the right, which places your foot on the little toe edge.

In the same manner as above, slide the foot on that edge until fully extended, and then rotate it to the flat foot before returning.

Repeat several times.

Widen the stance; drop the right knee in toward the center of the body, which places the foot on the big-toe edge.

While on that edge, slide the foot out to its full extension, rotate it to flatness and return it to the original position.

Repeat several times.

Do this entire process with the left leg and foot.

Extend both legs and feet and gently rotate each entire leg in and out several times.

This entire process can be repeated with each foot while pushing the hip forward with the leg extension. Note that you don't twist the torso or pull it back when you extend the leg and foot. Allow the hips and pelvis to be the initiators of the movement. Lead with the hip when pulling back to the original position. You might need to hold on to the edge of the chair to keep from sliding off as you do these extensions.

Arms

Lower back problems can often be traced to tensed, held shoulders and arms. These exercises can be done while sitting or standing.

Allow one arm to hang at your side, turn the thumb forward, and extend the arm.

Once extended, turn the palm down and allow the arm to return.

Repeat, but this time, turn the thumb in toward the body and extend the arm forward.

Once extended, turn the thumb out (so palm is upward), then return the arm to the side.

Repeat while extending the arm diagonally across the body. Keep the elbow straight, but not locked.

Turn the thumb alternately in and out.

Next, extend the arm diagonally behind you.

Again, turn the thumb in and out.

Release to the side.

Repeat the entire process with the opposite arm.

A key to all of this work is an Alexander Technique principle, which is to consciously direct the neck to be free as you work with any exercise. Remember that thought can innervate muscle and thinking of freeing the neck can bring about release of tension in the neck.

CONCEPTS OF SPACE AND PROCESSES OF CREATION EXERCISES

Clustering

Clustering is a nonlinear brainstorming technique akin to spontaneous free association, which forms the centerpiece of Gabriele Rico's excellent book *Writing the Natural Way.*[8] Because words, images, and ideas emanate from a central core and branch out in long tendrils of thought, it is possible to trace the structural linkage of ideas as they chain together. It is a marvelous way to begin gathering ideas around a word or an image and then to follow the path of a brainstorm as it gathers momentum, changes direction, and intensifies. You can use this technique to explore any word, image, name, or concept at any time in the writing process. If you are exploring your associations with a particular character, start with that character's name. If you are playing with theme, find a word that expresses that idea most fully and start there.

Clustering begins with a word or image in the center of a blank piece of paper (see Figure 1–1).

Allow the mind to freely associate with that word or image and write responses in chains of connected ideas (see Figure 1–2).

Figure 1–1. Central image or idea

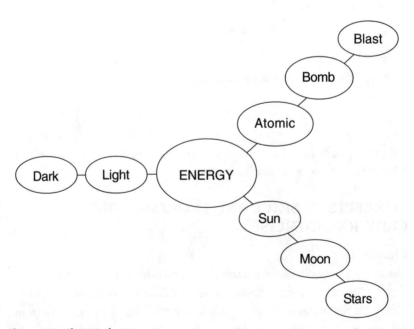

Figure 1–2. Cluster chains

Connect the words in a single chain with a line or series of lines radiating outward like a spider web. When one chain of thought runs out, start another one, returning back to the original word or image. Don't stop writing. The chief word here is *allow*. Let the writing control your hand, your thought, your response. *Don't stop.* When the cluster is done, you will know it. The energy will simply run out and there will be a sense of completion, a feeling that it is done.

The Click

At some point in the writing you may experience what I call the click, a felt sense of a shift of energy, concentration, direction, or focus. This is an emotional connection that has more heat than other chains of ideas. There is a quickening of thought, which is often reflected in the web itself: one chain may be longer than the others or may contain more provocative imagery, greater contrast, or more intensity. Your handwriting may become messier in your haste to follow the feeling. You will know if you have experienced a click or not, but others may also be able to hear it in the voice of the writing as well. (See Figure 1–3, p. 18.)

The Vignette

The second stage of clustering is now to gather the fragments of ideas, images, thoughts, and feelings into some kind of organized structure that has a beginning, middle, and end. If you have experienced a click, that is often a good place to begin. A vignette is a short piece that incorporates some or all of the material generated in the cluster. It may take any form: a free verse or metered poem, description, narrative, monologue, dialogue or scene. It could also be a short piece of composed or choreographed movement based on a theme and variations that follow the form and feeling of the individual chains.

The Vignette

The energy of light in the darkness

of suns and stars

caught in the heaven of your hands,

reaching to hold me in your heart

forever . . .

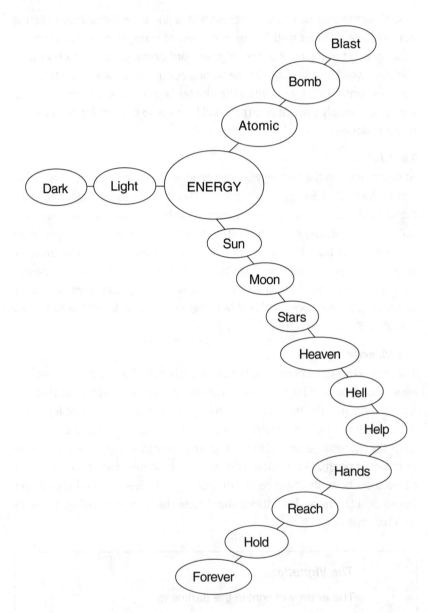

Figure 1–3. The click

Space Exercise

1. Draw a blueprint, diagram, or drawing of the space where you most often do your creative work. Be sure to consider the following:

   surroundings (colors, textures, furniture, objects)

   ambient elements (sounds, food, TV, other people)

   usual time (morning, evening, late at night)

   how you inhabit the space (sitting, standing, lying down)

   emotional dynamics (calm or stressed?)

2. Draw a blueprint, diagram, or drawing of your ideal writing space.
3. Consider the differences between your ideal space and your actual space.

   What prevents you from realizing the ideal?

   What changes might you make to make your actual space more ideal?

   What prevents you from doing this?

Process Exercise

1. Think back on an extended developmental period you have had with a specific play or project that typifies your working process.

   Try to reconnect with your first impulse or flash of insight.

   Remember how you fed this idea with specific images, ideas or research.

   What emotions did you go through in this initial gestation?

   What flashes of illumination occurred? When? Why?

   Who else was involved in the developmental process?

   What kinds of developmental structures did you use? (readings; workshops; meetings with dramaturg, director, actors; production)

   Which parts of the process were most/least helpful?

   Which parts of the process did you most/least enjoy?

2. Draw a time line or graphic representation of this process. Do *not* use any words, only images and symbols.

   Try to capture the emotional dynamics of the process as clearly as you can.

3. As you look at this drawing, try to decide what parts of the process you might have changed if you had had the opportunity to do so.

A WORD OR TWO . . .

The movement exercises that you will find throughout this book may be done in the privacy of your own space or in a class, workshop, or writing group with someone leading you through the activities. If this is not possible, I encourage you to record the instructions with ample pauses for execution and to play them back so that you can follow them while listening. It is difficult indeed to try to read and move at the same time.

The writing exercises that follow each chapter are designed to allow you to put the concepts in each chapter into practice in your work in your own way. Most can be done either as solo writing prompts or in a class, workshop, or writing group.

NOTES

1. Gaston Bachelard, *The Poetics of Space: The Classic Look at How We Experience Intimate Places*, trans. Maria Jolas (Boston: Beacon Press, 1994), x.

2. Carl Jung, *Man and His Symbols* (New York: Dell, 1964), 175.

3. Victor Shklovsky, "Art as Technique," *in Russian Formalist Criticism; Four Essays, trans. Lee T. Lemon and Marion J. Reis* (Lincoln: University of Nebraska Press, 1965), 12.

4. Gay McAuley, *Space in Performance: Making Meaning in Theater* (Ann Arbor: University of Michigan Press, 1999).

5. Howard Gardner, *Creating Minds: An Anatomy of Creativity as Seen Through the Lives of Freud, Einstein, Picasso, Stravinsky, Eliot, Graham, and Gandhi* (New York: Basic, 1993).

6. Vera John-Steiner, *Creative Collaboration* (New York: Oxford University Press, 2000).

7. Betty Edwards, *Drawing on the Artist Within* (New York: Simon and Schuster, 1986), 2–5, 46–47.

8. Gabriele Rico, *Writing the Natural Way: Using Right Brain Techniques to Release Your Expressive Powers* (Los Angeles: J. P. Tarcher, 1983).

2

CHAPTER

Child Space

OUR FIRST EXPERIENCE OF CREATION TAKES PLACE APPROXIMATELY nine months before the moment of our birth, in that instant when one bit of someone connects with another bit of someone else and starts a process that will eventually lead us to ourselves. Our earliest experience of space is that of oneness with an environment in which every element exists solely for our nurture and support. In the relative safety of the womb, we have all space and no space. Time is measured by our own bodies as we develop eyes and organs and fingers and toes. We dwell at the center of our own universe, quietly growing from nothing into something and from something into someone. When we are suddenly propelled into the world as thinking, feeling, sensing beings, there is a radical change in time and space. We find ourselves in an environment fraught with danger. For many months after our birth, we cannot distinguish between our own bodies and the surrounding environment. Our eyes do not focus; our senses are not localized in space. But as our bodies develop and sensory motor skills increase to allow movement, our world expands as we see and smell and taste and feel it.

LITERAL AND METAPHORIC CHILD SPACE

For the artist, child space is both literal and metaphoric. In the literal domain of our actual childhood, there are memories of people and events, sounds, smells, and tastes, which are ours to draw upon. Poets, playwrights, painters, and philosophers have always woven the strands of their childhoods into the fabric of their art. Whether Tennessee Williams, Eugene O'Neill, and Lillian Hellman drew upon these sources consciously or unconsciously, childhood ghosts and phantoms haunt their plays in characters, themes, and plots. Some writers create out of a deeply sub-merged sense of the abandoned child, constantly seeking what they longed for but never found, while others celebrate an idealized childhood that may or may not correspond to the actual childhood they lived.

Equally important is the metaphoric childhood that we abstract from our specific experience of childhood into a sense of wonder and discovery. This is the child space that is always within us no matter what our age. It is the place where childlike capacities for curiosity and spontaneity allow creative connections to be made without the censorship of an adult perspective that is bound by the rules and limitations of the "right" way to do something. The processes of deeply creative work often replicate the natural patterns of the ways very young children play, learn, and experience the world. Their entire beings are engaged in thinking, feeling, sensing, and moving. They play with concepts and ideas and make discoveries almost by accident in ways that are often surprising.

In my own work as a playwright, I have explored child space for almost thirty years, mostly through the eyes of the young protagonists who populate my plays. The child characters I have written have challenged me to find their depth and dignity in ways that are both subtle and profound. But there are deeper reasons for writers to spend a bit of time with their own literal and metaphoric child space. The ways in which children perceive their environment, learn about their world, and express themselves in imaginative play are fundamental to an understanding of adult creativity. As writers, our powers of expression are intricately tied to the ways in which we perceive, conceptualize, and represent the world around us. All too often we pass through our days with our senses dulled by familiarity and habit, to the point that we actually cease to see what is around us. The next time you are around a group of very young children, watch the ways they explore an unfamiliar space with a wild explosion of energy—running, crawling, touching, and sometimes even tasting their surroundings. It is possible for us to recapture that essence, at any age, but it takes a bit of "unknowing." It is, therefore, useful for us to go back to the beginning and to examine the ways in which we learned to learn through the daily discovery of our own capacities.

FROM CHILD DEVELOPMENT TO ADULT CREATIVITY

At birth, the right and left hemispheres of a baby's brain are in close proximity, separated by the corpus callosum, a cortex of 200 million nerve fibers that connect and separate the two halves of the brain. In her book *Writing the Natural Way*, Gabriele Rico suggests that our phenomenal ability to learn in infancy and early childhood may have something to do with the fact that the two brains do not seem to interfere with each other's mode of learning. Some neurologists have hypothesized that during infancy, before we acquire language, the right brain is dominant, organizing images and experiences into meaningful patterns, finding conceptual wholeness and emotional nuances in the surrounding world. As language skills develop, the left brain focuses on the specific and individual meanings and we begin to recognize signs and symbols made manifest in words. Over the next eleven years, the corpus callosum will develop, and the brain will become fully lateralized with constant communication between the two halves. In most cases the left brain, with its emphasis on linear sequence, logic, and information, will become dominant. But in infancy, communication between the right and left hemispheres is not a long-distance call.[1]

An instinct for dramatic play, the joy of movement, and self-expression in drawing all came naturally to us when we were children. These forms of expression were our natural teachers. They helped us organize our world and tell stories to ourselves about ourselves. We moved for the pleasure of movement because it felt good to spin in circles and to run as fast as we could run. When we became adults, we organized movement into sports with rules; spontaneous play became planned exercise with goals and objectives. The point of basketball became beating the other team, not the pure physical joy of running and leaping.

When we were children, the joy of drawing was, at first, the physical sensation of scribbling. Gradually, we tried to represent the world around us in visual form, drawing bodies as blobs with dots for eyes and semicircles for mouths. As our sense of proportion developed, we made long sausage figures with shortened torsos, impossibly long legs, and big eyes and noses, which was the way we often saw adults peering down at us. As we grew older, what the drawing was "supposed to be" became more important than what it was. Just as the rules of the game turned the joy of movement into sports, the rules of literal depiction turned naturally abstract art into conventional representation. All too often, as we gained skill it was at the expense of imagination. If we can each find within ourselves the girl who used to tell epic stories with finger paint and the boy who created and destroyed whole worlds with the stroke of a crayon, these children have much to teach us.

Recent research into creativity in later life reveals that the same characteristics of joyful inquiry, freedom to take risks, and the ability to explore multiple domains of expression that are present in the learning and play of children are also the main ways that older people continue to be vitally engaged in creative activity well into their eighties and nineties. A key seems to be the involvement of the entire psychophysical self and a willingness to approach every new undertaking as a beginner, excited by what is unknown rather than inhibited by preconceptions of limitations.[2]

WRITING FROM THE CHILD SPACE

The writer has two childhoods from which to draw: the factual past and the remembered past. Although they are both based on the same source, the child space of memory may be quite different from factual childhood. Gaston Bachelard writes, "It is on the plane of daydreams and not that of facts that childhood remains alive and poetically useful within us."[3] The factual memory of childhood disappears into an imaginal memory imbued with images, wishes, longings, and desires that have been with us since we were small. This is not to say that historical accuracy is not important, particularly if you are writing a memoir or autobiography, but for most artists it is the remembered mother, the longed-for or resented mother, rather than the biological mother, that resonates with an audience or reader.

For the writer, an honest and unflinching exploration of child space can reap rich rewards for you and for the characters who inhabit your plays and stories. This is particularly true for crafting young characters, children or adolescents, who are often thinly portrayed and heavily stereotyped. Some playwrights are hesitant or unable to write fully dimensional child characters and rely on a very limited range of types: the bratty child, the wise child, the nerd, and the bully. The best way to write a child character is to forget that he or she is a child and to concentrate on what makes this person unique in his or her life experience, imagination, vocabulary, and so on. It can also be useful to explore the fictional childhoods of your adult characters. Although the details of their biographies may never actually appear in the play, you will have a deeper, more richly detailed psychological understanding of them as adults if you have some idea of the forces that formed them.

A recent student of mine working on a play about the devastating impact of incest had to get back to a time in the life of his protagonist when she felt her father had actually loved her. Although the character is in middle age at the time of the play, the playwright made important connections through the exploration of that character's child space.

It can also be very useful for writers to mine the resources of their own literal childhoods for material built of memory. The conscious exploration of the child space from the vantage point of the adult is often highly charged with emotional energy. Even the most seemingly placid memories can stir up deep and unexpected responses in retrospect. Students in my classes are often astonished at the tears that come unbidden in a visualization of their child selves or at the memory of the house in which they grew up. For some people child space is filled with land mines, secrets, and psychological and physical pain; for others, even happy memories have intense emotional dimensions. Remember, however, that any voyage into the past should be taken with care and in a controlled environment, as there is a fine line between exploration and therapy.

Although I believe that all creative expression is inherently therapeutic, it is not the intention of this work to take the place of professional therapy. Therapy seeks out the pathology of the past and focuses attention on those areas that cause the most physical and psychic pain in order to work through the causes of that pain to find some release. The writer's exploration of the child space is intended to open the doors to childhood memories, but it is up to the individual whether or not to cross the threshold. The purpose is not confrontation, but access. Actors understand that emotional involvement is absolutely crucial to the expression of their art, but writers are sometimes less comfortable with their own emotions than with those of their characters. It is the safety of this emotional distance that allows them to risk writing about highly charged material. This must always be respected.

In the years that I have been exploring the child space for myself as a writer and with my students, I have radically altered my conception of time from a linear concept to a simultaneous one. I have come to believe that chronology is an illusion that we have created out of a need for order in the universe to give us the security of a fixed point in time and space. But that is not the way we experience time or space in our minds and bodies. The past is not just memory, but a perpetual presence. Instead of a time line, I offer the analogy of a tree. The youth of the tree is the sapling that always lives at the center as the tree ages and puts on rings of experience. Each ring represents a period of time and contains all that has happened to the tree. Some rings are thicker, reflecting good growth in times of plenty; some are thinner, representing times of drought. A blackened ring indicates a forest fire survived. No matter how tall the tree becomes, or how many years are counted out in concentric circles, the youth of the tree is still alive at its center. The growth and vitality of the tree demands the perpetual presence of its childhood as a source of nourishment and support.

The same holds true for us. Even if childhood was a time of trial and pain, it has formed us in deep and subtle ways. We hold within our minds and muscles the rings of our experience. No matter what our chronological age, our child space always resides within us as a place of comfort or of crises. At every age, we are every age we have ever been and, perhaps, every age we will ever be.

The exercises included in this chapter may be done in the privacy of your own study or in a group setting like a workshop or a classroom. They should be undertaken with some caution, particularly if they are done in a group setting. The leader must remain sensitive to any members of the group who seem to lose emotional control or who react with passivity or anger. The leader should never push any point or demand that participants go deeper than their comfort level. Several of the exercises call for physical interaction between participants. Some students have expressed discomfort with being asked to put their heads in a partner's lap and to make eye contact. Everyone has a different level of personal comfort with physical interaction, and a leader must remain sensitive to this fact.

Be particularly sensitive to sharing results of these activities and exercises. While some may be eager to share what they have written, others may feel it is too revealing. Pressuring participants to read what might be sensitive material can damage trust and make individuals feel vulnerable and exposed just when they need to feel safe and protected. At the same time, just as emotional response is appropriate and indeed necessary in an acting class, the presence of emotion during these activities signals a level of involvement that is desirable. The presence of the past within the present is a powerful experience. For some, the whole idea of returning to the child space is overwhelming and should not be taken lightly or casually; for others, it is a joyous journey of rejuvenation and renewal.

MOVEMENT: DEVELOPMENTAL MOVEMENT

The purpose of the physical work in this chapter is twofold: first, to allow you to reexperience the physiological developmental patterns of your early childhood and, second, to reawaken a sense of release and the joy of movement.

Remember the reckless abandon of throwing a tantrum or the soaring elation of playing airplane, arms outstretched, zooming down a sidewalk or across a polished floor? These are forms of Developmental Movement. We came to this work through Jim's experience with helping actors realize that their habitual movement patterns, behavioral gestures, and even the structural components of their bodies were strongly influenced by early childhood experiences and family modeling. His inquiry was deepened by the discovery of the Developmental Movement Techniques developed by Bonnie Bainbridge Cohen at the School for Body-Mind Centering in Amherst, Massachusetts.[4] The foundation of this work is the observation that most children go through a series of movement patterns as part of their normal sensory motor development. These patterns involve a progression from lying flat, to lifting arms and legs, to turning over, to raising the body up on the arms, to rocking, to crawling, to standing, to walking, and, eventually, to running, leaping, and so on. While this might seem obvious at first, more careful observation reveals that these commonplace activities are actually a delicately sequenced series of movements that involve four basic locomotor movement patterns: lateral movement (same side), contralateral movement (opposite sides), homologous movement (top to bottom and bottom to top), and spinal movement. Repetition of these patterns exercises all the major muscle groups, helps organize the nervous system, has an effect on glandular development, and may even have an impact upon brain chemistry.

When performed by adults, Developmental Movement can stimulate muscular, glandular, and even psychophysical response. Though the movements seem elementary to those of us who usually equate movement with dance or sports, they are actually very taxing. After ten minutes of crawling, young and robust college students are often exhausted. In contrast, a two-year-old is just getting warmed up. What is most astonishing is the effect this movement work has had upon writers, who have found that the repetitive patterns bring forth a host of memories and emotional responses. It is a commonly held misconception that memory is stored only in the brain. In fact, our muscles, skin cells, and all of the nerve endings in our bodies also store our memories. If writing is a complete use of the self in all of our physical, mental, and emotional complexities, then bringing out some of the movements of our earliest experience can put us in touch with parts of ourselves we thought we had left behind.

In order to experience these exercises, you must do them fully. You must try to recapture the sensation of doing these movements for the first time and forget that you already know how to walk when you crawl. An infant learns first through the muscles and then through the mind. As an adult, you must allow your body to teach you what you think you already know, in order to see what you can discover next. As an adult, you are also aware of physical limitations of age and injury. Some of the floor exercises here might be difficult or painful, particularly for those with lower back problems. Always use caution when undertaking *any* physical work, particularly if it is new to you.

Developmental Movement Exercises
Sun Ray Stretch 1

Stand on the floor with your feet slightly apart.

Place your arms above your head in a V and your legs in another V.

Stretch through both arms and both legs.

Radiate energy from the navel through the whole body.

Inhale as the energy builds.

Exhale as the energy shoots through the body.

Do these stretches four or five times to clear the mind.

Sun Ray Stretch 2

Lie on your back and place your arms above your head in a V and your legs in another V with the pelvis slightly titled toward the head, but not lifted off the floor. Take a moment to breathe and to consciously radiate energy from the navel through your whole body. Exhale as you lift and inhale as you release for each of the following.

Arm Lifts

Lift the right arm just enough to clear the floor.

Return it to the floor.

Repeat several times.

Lift the left arm just enough to clear the floor.

Return it to the floor.

Repeat several times.

Lift both arms at the same time.

Repeat the motion several times.

Release the arms back into the V position.

Leg Lifts

Lift the right leg just enough to clear the floor.

Return it to the floor.

Repeat several times.

Lift the left leg just enough to clear the floor.

Return it to the floor.

Repeat several times.

Lift both legs just enough to clear the floor; remember to tilt the pelvis toward the head.

Return the legs to the floor.

Repeat several times.

Arm and Leg Lifts

Lift right arm and leg together.

Lift left arm and leg together.

Repeat several times.

Lift right arm and left leg together. Repeat several times.

Lift left arm and right leg together. Repeat several times.

Lift both arms and legs together. Repeat several times.

Roll gently onto your stomach and place arms and legs in the V position.

Lift arms and legs together and stretch through the entire body.

Release your energy into the mat on the floor and imagine that you are flying through the clouds. Flying will reduce the effort of the exercise.

Reaching and Grasping

Roll over to your back. Pull your knees up so your feet are flat.

Raise arms up at a ninety-degree angle so that your shoulders are flat on the floor and your fingers are extended upward.

Reach up with your shoulder and then let it flop down again.

Imagine a rope reaching from your sternum to the ceiling.

Grasp the rope with your right hand, then with your left.

Reach and pull up the head and chest with a hand-over-hand motion.

Let yourself down, tilting your head toward your sternum.

Repeat this three to four times.

Pull your knees up until they are resting on the chest.

Stretch and bend knees in a bicycle motion.

Add the arms in the same bicycle motion.

Bicycle with the arms only, leaving the legs at rest.

Bicycle with the legs only, leaving the arms at rest.

Switch back and forth. Repeat three to four times.

Rocking

Roll onto your stomach and push up to your hands and knees.

Place your hands directly under your shoulders, keeping your body well supported. Rock forward and back.

Walk arms out a little and rock all the way forward and back.

Walk arms farther forward. Rock.

Sit back as far as possible. Rock.

Roll forward and flop back, resting your bottom on your heels.

Sit in a cross-legged position with your hands beside you.

Bend your elbows and rock from side to side.

Allow your head to go with the movement from side to side.

Rock from side to side for a minute or so.

Raising Up and Wriggling

Lie on your stomach, breathe in through your nose, and release each breath through your mouth.

Explore how to raise yourself. How do you push yourself up?

Perhaps you might bend your right leg, extend your left arm over your head, roll over, and push back.

Repeat with the other side.

Using only your arms and shoulders, find a way to move forward and back.

Wriggle on your belly like a reptile!

Crawling

Lie on your stomach and push up with your arms.

Roll back until you are curled up onto your heels.

Push up to hands and knees with your head leading.

Flop back to your heels.

Repeat this several times.

Begin to crawl. Go forward. Go backward.

Crawl around for a while, moving forward and back.

Crawl using the arm and leg on the same side.

Now, switch and crawl using opposite arms and legs.

Alternate using same and opposite sides.

Crawl for several minutes. Be careful of any undue stress on the knees. It is best to practice crawling on a soft surface.

Walking and Beyond

From a crawling position, explore how you might get to your feet.

Perhaps put one foot on the floor under you and hoist yourself up using a wall or chair for balance.

Are there other ways?

Test your precarious balance slowly.

Follow where the weight of your head leads you as you begin to move.

Stagger about for a bit, testing speed and balance.

This movement can evolve from walking, to running, to leaping.

Extend your arms.

Make the sounds of a motor.

Fly!

Tantrum

Lie down on your back with your knees up and your arms at your sides, palms up.

Press into the floor so that your knees flop from side to side and your head follows slowly and easily.

Repeat several times.

Lift your right forearm, bending at the wrist, and lift up onto the elbow at a ninety-degree angle.

Allow your arm to drop back down as your palm slaps the floor.

Do not hurt your palm or your arm.

Repeat this with the left arm.

Alternate arms.

Lift the right foot slightly off the floor and then allow it to drop down again.

Use the entire sole of the foot.

Do not bang your heel on the floor.

Lift the left foot slightly off the floor and then allow it to drop down again.

Alternate right foot and then left foot.

Repeat lifting the arms and feet all together and allowing them to drop down again.

Alternate.

Together.

Alternate.

Pound on the floor with your feet and hands. Add sound.

Have a *tantrum*!

After the release of the *tantrum*, allow your breath to come in easy "ha ha" sounds.

If laughter comes, allow it.

If tears come, allow them.

Both laughter and tears are spontaneous energy releases. Allow for the cleansing energy of both!

CHILD SPACE EXERCISES

Some of the exercises in this chapter may be done as solo activities in the solitude of your own writing space or as group activities for a class or workshop. In either format, you may do these exercises for yourself as a means of reconnecting with your own childhood, or you may assume the point of view of a character in a play you are working on and complete the exercise from that point of view. The details of a fictional childhood for your character may never appear in a play, but they will add emotional texture and depth simply because you have considered them. Whether you do these exercises for yourself or for your character, the chief word here is *allow*. Do not judge, edit, or censor yourself. Do not place an adult expectation on what the result should be. Sit in a quiet place and try to clear your mind of unnecessary clutter. It might help to have a timer nearby so you can respond to each of the prompts by writing for about a minute. When the timer goes off, go on to the next prompt. In the eye of your mind, hold an image either of yourself as a child or of your character as a child. Try to see this image in as much detail as possible.

If you do these activities in a group setting, remember that for some people this material is highly emotionally charged, and for others it is not. Both responses are fine. The following activity was created by Jean Houston in her excellent book *The Possible Human.*[5] Although it is presented here as a group activity to be done in pairs, it is equally provocative as a journaling experience or a solo writing activity. What is most important is that the writer feels a sense of safety and comfort in exploring this material. For some this is best accomplished in the privacy of their own writing space; for others the group setting is liberating.

Priming the Memory Bank

One of you will lie down and the other will sit by that person's head and say the following, allowing about two minutes or so for each response.

Tell me from your childhood . . .

> about a very young boy
>
> about an old lady
>
> about your favorite foods
>
> about a much loved or hated teacher
>
> about eating an ice-cream cone
>
> about your bedroom as a child
>
> about climbing a tree
>
> about what you ate for breakfast
>
> about a pair of shoes you wore
>
> about a family trip

Now reverse roles so that the person who was lying down will ask the questions and the one who was sitting will lie down and respond to the following suggestions.

Tell me from your childhood . . .

about a balloon

about going to the store

about going to the beach or playing in water

about songs you sang or heard; sing one of these songs now

about a birthday party

about blowing bubble gum

about a very young girl

about an old man

about interesting smells that you remember

about a character from radio, TV, or the movies

Now stand up and see how you feel. How does your body feel? Your head?

After both partners have had the opportunity to share memories, the facilitator should encourage the participants to take a moment to silently review all of the images, impressions, people, places, and moments that have come to the surface of consciousness.

Allow one image to select itself, one that is particularly vibrant.

Tag that memory with a single word.

Write the word in the center of a clean sheet of paper.

Cluster the word.

Write a vignette based on the cluster.

If this exercise is done in a group, please remember that the experience is likely to be very intense, particularly for writers who are often solo creators and do not usually place themselves in situations where they are required to make physical contact or to share intimate details from their real lives. Always invite those who might not be comfortable to participate as a solo writing activity and/or to do this activity from the point of view of a character they are writing about rather than themselves.

Drawing the House of Your Childhood

This activity can be done as a solo activity or in a group; it may also be done for yourself or for a character. Simply adjust the point of view accordingly. If you are doing the exercise for yourself, read through the visualization section and then follow the directions for the drawing. In a group, a facilitator will lead the participants through the visualization and give directions for the drawing.

Visualization

Let your mind go back to the house or apartment of your childhood. Maybe it's the first house you remember or the house you see in your dreams.

See the house or apartment in as much detail as you can.

See it first from a distance, as though you are standing on the street looking at it.

Slowly approach, taking note of the neighborhood, the yard, and so on.

Walk up the path or down the corridor.

The front door is open and you go in.

Take a few moments to explore the rooms:

Attend to what you see, hear, smell, taste, and feel.

Attend to the colors, textures, and shapes.

See the furniture, lighting fixtures, wallpaper, and carpets.

Are there any people in your house? If so, where are they?

When you have finished exploring the house, go outside; continue to explore the yard or surrounding area.

Move away from the house and look back at it.

Say good-bye to that space and let it go from your memory.

Drawing

Use a pencil and clean piece of paper and draw the floor plan of the house you have just visited.

Draw in the size and shape and arrangement of the various rooms.

Include windows and doors, corridors, and so on.

This is how you remember the space, not necessarily a scale architectural drawing.

Find your place in this house, the place of your greatest feeling of oneness, solitude, and belonging.

Draw yourself in that space.

Draw in the furniture, particularly the pieces that have special significance.

If there are people that you remember associated with this room or space, draw them in.

If there are significant events associated with this room or space, draw in the memory of those events.

The experience of the drawing is more important than the product of the drawing!

Sharing (if in a group setting)
The facilitator asks everyone to find and to sit opposite a partner.

Make some kind of physical contact.

A closes his or her eyes while B takes A on a guided tour of the house of his or her childhood, filling in as much detail as possible. A visualizes the images described.

Attend to all sensory details in each room.

Pay particular attention to how each space feels.

Switch, so that the guide is now the tourist and the tourist is now the guide.

Now look at the drawings and see how they compare with the spaces visualized.

The Book of Time
This activity can also be done as solo writing or in a group. If you are working with it by yourself, read through the visualization section, taking time to form these images in your mind. At the end of each section, write down the message given to you by the child self. If this is done in a group, participants should lie comfortably on the floor or on a mat and the leader should take them through the visualization at a comfortable pace. We have found that unobtrusive music playing softly during the visualization is very effective.

It should be noted that this exercise often produces a very strong emotional reaction. If this activity is done in a group setting, be sure that the group members have developed trust with each other and with the leader. Throughout the exercise, watch the responses of the participants carefully. Tears are not necessarily a bad thing, but if someone appears to be having a difficult time, a reassuring touch on the shoulder or a deftly given tissue can be very helpful.

Visualization

You see before you a book of time. In that book are photographs from your entire life, and the page that you are open to now is your present age.

As you turn the page back one year, suddenly you are there again, feeling what you felt then, knowing only what you knew then and nothing more. You turn back one page at a time, going back fully and completely in each year.

Keep turning until you see a photograph of yourself as teenager.

Notice details of the picture.

Notice who is in it and what they are doing.

Step through the frame of the photograph.

Enter the photograph as yourself at your present age and watch the activity.

You are invisible. Observe the interaction. Listen to what is going on.

Gradually all others in the photograph begin to disappear, leaving only the teenage self and you.

Approach the teenage self and make contact.

The teenage self has a message for you.

Receive the message. (*If you are doing this exercise alone, take a moment to write down the message.*)

Step back through the frame of the photograph. Let it go.

Keep turning until you see a photograph of yourself as a young child, five to six years old.

Notice details of the picture.

Notice who is in it and what they are doing.

Step through the frame of the photograph.

Enter the photograph as yourself at your present age and watch the activity.

You are invisible. Observe the interaction. Listen to what is going on.

Gradually all others in the photograph begin to disappear, leaving only the child self and you.

Approach the child self and make contact.

The child self has a message for you.

Receive the message. (*If you are doing this exercise alone, take a moment to write down the message.*)

Step back through the frame of the photograph. Let it go.

Keep turning until you see a photograph of yourself as a baby less than one year old.

Notice details of the picture.

Notice who is in it and what they are doing.

Step through the frame of the photograph.

Enter the photograph as yourself at your present age and watch the activity.

You are invisible. Observe the interaction. Listen to what is going on.

Gradually all others in the photograph begin to disappear, leaving only the infant self and you. Approach the infant self; hold that baby in your arms.

The infant self has a message for you.

You can understand the message just by looking into the infant's eyes.

You understand it perfectly.

Receive the message. (*If you are doing this exercise alone, take a moment to write down the message.*)

Hold the infant close; feel your hearts beating as one.

Step back through the frame of the photograph.

Let it go.

After you have met all three selves (the teenage self, the child self, and the infant self) and have heard their messages, remember those words and select one message that seems particularly important to you now.

Write down the message in a word or short phrase.

Cluster the message.

Allow the cluster to take whatever direction it takes.

Be sensitive to the click.

Write a conversation between the teenage, child, or infant self and the adult you are now.

Write a vignette based upon the cluster and/or the conversation.

It may be a scene between the child self and you.

It may be a poem, narrative, dialogue, or monologue.

Allow it to take whatever form it wants to take.

Another variation on this exercise is to actually construct the book of time, by drawing the images in the photographs or by finding photos in magazines or on the Internet. This can be particularly helpful if you are making one for a character you are creating. The images can be impressions of that character at various times throughout his or her life. Working in a visual medium can be *such* a relief from writing.

A WORD OR TWO . . .

Once when I was in an office supply store buying a folder to contain a play I had written about Sherlock Holmes, the clerk at the checkout told me he had seen a movie about Sherlock's childhood. I nodded and smiled, as I too had seen *The Young Sherlock Holmes.*

"Was that really true?" he asked me.

"Was what really true?" I replied.

"That movie. Did all that really happen?"

As deftly as I could, I explained that Sherlock Holmes was a literary character and never really had a childhood, to which he replied, "Are you sure?"

Whether you use these exercises for your characters or for yourself, do so with the joy of not knowing where this journey might take you. The time you spend in the literal or metaphoric playground of childhood cannot help but enrich this present moment.

NOTES

1. Gabriele Rico, *Writing the Natural Way: Using Right Brain Techniques to Release Your Expressive Powers* (Los Angeles: J. P. Tarcher, 1983) 73–74.

2. Jeanne Nakamura and Mihaly Csikszentmihalyi, "Creativity in Later Life," in *Creativity and Development*, ed. R. Keith Sawyer (New York: Oxford University Press, 2003), 186–213.

3. Gaston Bachelard, *The Poetics of Space: The Classic Look at How We Experience Intimate Places*, trans. Maria Jolas (Boston: Beacon, 1994) 16.

4. For more information about Developmental Movement, see *Sensing, Feeling and Action*, by Bonnie Bainbridge Cohen (Northampton: Contact Collaborations, 1994) and *Developmental Movement Therapy*, by Bonnie Bainbridge Cohen and Margret Mills (Amherst, MA: School for Body-Mind Centering, 1979), or www.bodymindcentering.com.

5. Jean Houston, *The Possible Human: A Course in Enhancing Your Physical, Mental, and Creative Abilities* (Los Angeles: J. P. Tarcher, 1982), 88–89.

3
CHAPTER

Psychophysical Space

IN THIS CHAPTER WE WILL EXAMINE NOTIONS OF SPACE CONTAINED within the boundaries of our own minds and bodies, paying particular attention to the forces that create tension, motion, balance, and imbalance. The term *psychophysical space* refers to how our minds and bodies perceive space and how those perceptions shape the way we organize our reality in terms of physical phenomena, emotional states, and moral and ethical concepts. The tensional forces that exist within our bodies and the surrounding environment mirror the tensional forces that bring depth and complexity to the characters we create, the stories we spin, and the themes and issues we explore in writing.

In this chapter we shall experience these tensional forces physically through movement, visually through abstract drawing, and verbally by giving voice to emotional states and abstract representations of the forces within characters and plays. This work begins in the connection between body and mind. In this context it is important to distinguish between mind and brain. The brain is the center of the nervous system. It is the command central of all of our bodily functions, from heartbeat and breath, to sensory motor control, to language development, to emotional response. The mind, however, is a somewhat broader concept and serves as the center of consciousness that generates thoughts, feelings, ideas, and perceptions. The mind stores knowledge and memory, makes meaning, creates understanding, and places value. Psychophysical space is the territory shared between mind and body, where ideas are born and images are formed.

SELF-USE

Actors and dancers are keenly aware of their psychophysical selves because they depend on the physical reality of their bodies as the primary instrument of communication. These artists realize that they must train body and mind to work together to provide ease and economy of motion, to sharpen sensory awareness, and to deepen emotional availability. Writers, however, tend to see their work as somehow outside of themselves, as residing in an idea, image, character, or plot that is somehow separate from its creator. Although the initial process of conception is perhaps more personal and intimate for writers than it is for performers, actors and dancers embody their craft, whereas writers generally work out of themselves into their craft. Training for actors and dancers centers on their bodies and voices and their ability to depict emotional states with truth and intensity. Training for writers tends to focus on techniques of building character, developing plot, refining language, articulating theme, and so on. For the performer, the ability to portray a wide variety of characters or to execute complicated choreography begins and ends with self-use. The paradox of performance lies in the actor's or dancer's ability to be free of habitual or unconscious movement and speech patterns, to literally transform into an "other." Only in the knowledge and understanding of the self can the other be found.

A writer rarely thinks of self-use in the same way. The body-mind connection is much less obvious, as the physical act of writing seems a sedentary process. Sitting in a chair for hours on end and staring at a computer screen or scribbling page after page by hand hardly seem to be aerobic activities. But the writer's imaginal world is filled with movement: the physical actions of the plot, the emotional velocity of characters in conflict, the collision of ideas, and the linguistic gymnastics of words and images all contribute to the momentum of what we call dramatic action. The act of creation involves feeling, sensing, thinking, and movement, all of which are active rather than passive. Understandings of tensional forces, movement, and balance are as important to the writer as they are to the performer. But these principles must be experienced fully in the body for this knowledge to be of use. Mind and body are one, whole and indivisible.

SELF AND SPACE

Although different cultures use, divide, and conceive of space differently, there are certain cross-cultural similarities that occur with remarkable consistency. Chief among them is the fact that fundamental principles of spatial organization relate directly to the posture and structure of the upright human body. Our bodies in space provide the focal point for our concepts of direction, location, and distance. In his book *Space and Place*, geographer Yi-Fu Tuan points out that among mammals, human beings are unique in that they easily maintain an upright position. As we stand, space surrounds us and is differentiated into that which lies ahead and behind, to the right and to the left, above and below us. Although we often speak of our space as being three-dimensional, it has, in fact, six dimensions. The polarities of up and down, front and back, right and left have cultural connotations with far-reaching implications. The way we perceive ourselves in space is a major determining factor in the ways we construct our concept of reality, not just physically, but emotionally and ethically as well.[1]

POLARITIES

High and *low*, the two poles of the vertical axis, are strongly charged words in most languages. Conceptually speaking, an upward direction has positive associations of elevated status, high moral and ethical standards, uplifting cultural values, elevated thoughts, and all the finer things to which we aspire. A downward direction, on the other hand, carries negative associations of lower status, base desires, depraved values, and depression. Below the surface of the conscious mind, the unconscious and subconscious are often associated with fears and phobias. We reach upward toward the light or fall down into darkness.

In addition to the vertical axis of up and down, there are psychological and cultural associations to the directions of front and back. Frontal space is primarily visual and seems to be much larger and more vivid than the space behind us. The space behind us is mysterious, dark, hidden, even dangerous. Our experience of time is also conditioned by body orientation. Frontal space is the future and contains our dreams, hopes, and plans while back space is the province of memory, as it holds the past in its domain.

The same physical, psychological, and cultural connotations also extend to concepts of right and left. Tuan tells us, "In nearly all cultures for which information is available, the right side is regarded as superior to the left."[2] The right side carries associations of correctness, power, strength, and dominance while the left side is considered to be nondominant, weaker, and somehow incorrect. In many kinds of physical and therapeutic practices, the right and left sides of the body present different kinds of energy identified with gender connotations. In chiropractics and polarity therapies, the right side of the body is associated with male energies, which hold tension and are expressed in action and aggression. The left side of the body is often associated with female energy, which is thought to be yielding, nondirective and releasing. These labels have less to do with biological gender than with cultural assumptions about gender, but they also reflect a tendency to polarize concepts into sharply differentiated categories. This same duality can be found in Chinese philosophy in principles of yin (darkness, negativity, and femininity) and yang (principles of light, heat, and masculinity). Wholeness comes not in the superiority or dominance of one mode over another, but in the balance between the two. Indeed the Chinese symbol for yin/yang is a single circle that holds both light and dark spheres, which flow one into the other in perfect harmony and balance.

TENSIONAL FORCES

Despite these cultural distinctions between the polarities of up and down, front and back, and right and left, one direction or polarity is not better or worse than the other; it is the interplay between them that is important. In our work as playwrights, we are constantly striving for the kind of complexity of character, plot, and theme that mirrors the interplay of the tensional forces we see in these polarities. A character is ethically complex when he or she embodies both positive and negative traits and exhibits conflicting desires, motivations, impulses, and inhibitions. This creates a tensional energy within the character. External forces that create conflict and exert pressure from the outside are important, too, but depth is achieved by finding those inner demons and desires that impel characters to action or drive them to despair. Hamlet is a great character because of his inconsistencies, not in spite of them. Lil' Bit in Paula Vogel's How I Learned to Drive is both attracted to and repelled by her incestuous Uncle Peck. She is both victim and aggressor, as is seen in the scene in which she attempts to seduce a teenager despite her own experiences with pedophilia. Her moral ambiguity is a measure of her strength as a character.

Tensional forces are particularly important in nontraditional plays that are not constructed in a linear fashion. Events need not be connected by cause and effect to create tension. In Caryl Churchill's surreal fantasy The Skriker, time functions as a tensional force as contemporary characters are juxtaposed against fantastical mythic phantoms in a life-and-death struggle over an unborn baby. The three women of Lisa D'Amour's fascinating Anna Bella Eema shapeshift from young girls to anguished mothers to werewolves to policemen to Frankenstein monsters at lightning speed. The tensional forces between conflicting identities and multiple perspectives create a state of imbalance that propels the action forward. The plays of Erik Ehn and Mac Wellman are wildly imagistic and linguistically complex. The tensional relationships between images, words, and ideas produce the sensation of forward momentum in a dizzying ride on a rhetorical roller coaster. Tensional forces cause movement, lead to action, and ultimately bring about a constant interaction between balance and imbalance. So it is with bodies in motion, and so it is with dramatic action.

BALANCE, IMBALANCE, AND DRAMATIC STRUCTURE

The traditional Aristotelian model of dramatic structure describes action as a series of events in which a state of stasis or balance is disrupted by an inciting event, which triggers a series of rising actions leading to a crisis, which causes a climax, which brings about a reversal leading to a falling action, which results in a new state of balance or stasis. The continual movement between balance, imbalance, and the struggle to regain balance provides momentum to a dramatic action. There is a constant tensional relationship between events. In linear, plot-driven plays, the relationship between events is usually cause and effect. One action causes the next, which triggers a reaction, which in turn causes the subsequent action. Most realistic plays follow this pattern. A causes B, which leads to C, and so on. The people of Thebes exhort Oedipus to find the cause of the plague destroying the city. Oedipus calls in the blind seer Teiresias; Teiresias tells Oedipus to be careful what he wishes for; Oedipus doesn't listen, and on it goes.

This constant interaction of balance and imbalance may be seen in plot construction, character development, and language patterns. This is particularly true in non-traditional, non-linear plays that defy the usual cause-and-effect relationships of Aristotelian structure. In his book *New Playwriting Strategies*, Paul Castagno calls contemporary language-based plays "polyvocal" in that "multiple language strategies and sources coexist in the play's characters and narratives, within a script containing diverse interests expressed in different speech forms."[3] These diverse elements create frisson, a thrilling tensional friction that brings about clashes between language and action and context in a way that disorients the audience:

> When language alters space and time, established moorings are loosened, as conventions are interrupted or displaced. The characters are de-centered, as is the audience, in a vertiginous environment. This

de-centering forces the character to make sense of an ever-changing theatrical landscape. The changing environmental factors create an interactive spatial/temporal field that is a dynamic contrast to conventional dramaturgy.[4]

Whether a play is traditional or nontraditional, linear or wildly episodic, tensional forces in plot, character, language, and theme and the constant interplay of balance and imbalance provide the heartbeat of dramatic action. In physics, as in life, balance is achieved when tensional forces are equally exerted upon a stationary object. When tensional energy is omnidirectional, coming from all six dimensions at once, the object in the center is not pulled in one direction or another. A state of balance in dramatic structure, as in life, is merely a moment, a pause, a blessed relief between episodes of conflict, tension, and stress. At the beginning of a play, a state of balance holds all of the elements of imbalance that await the trigger of an inciting event, image, or idea. At the end of a play, the new state of balance is always precarious because it contains all of the tensional forces necessary to set in motion the forces of the new play, the next play, the one that inevitability begins as soon as the old play has ended.

Several years ago a student of mine created a movement-based theatre piece titled *Weight* that explored concepts of balance and the tensional forces that exist between three characters: a mother, her daughter, and the mother's sister. Throughout the play all three characters were literally tied together with ropes and pulleys, shifting, testing, bearing, and releasing the weight of each other's bodies. The piece also explored the psychological relationships between these women and the constantly shifting tensions between them. The concept for the play was born in principles of physics and psychology. But the play itself could be found only in the body: first, in the body of the writer and, later, in the bodies of the actors.[5] Director Mary Zimmerman works in a similar manner. Her *Notebooks of Leonardo da Vinci* provides an excellent example of the theatrical use of psychophysical space. Virtually every word of the text is taken directly from the writings of da Vinci, but his rather abstract concepts of physics and philosophy are brought brilliantly to life through movement and in the physical relationships between the bodies of actors.

VISUAL METAPHOR

Psychophysical space is visual as well as kinesthetic. Tensional relationships and concepts of balance and imbalance may also be made manifest in drawing. In *Drawing on the Artist Within*, Betty Edwards suggests that the language of abstract drawing can clarify feeling states and concepts that because of their emotional complexity elude words. The visual elements of line, shape, color, texture, and composition, the use of positive and negative space, and the spatial arrangement of lines and shapes on the page form a vocabulary that permits precision and abstraction, boldness and delicacy, complexity and simplicity in a single image. For emotional states and tensional forces that are inherently paradoxical, a visual representation can effectively capture the essence of the contradiction without the need for reconciliation. Balance finds visual expression in symmetry, imbalance in asymmetry. Edwards calls this "analog drawing" because the sketches are analogous to the things they represent.[6]

Over the years I have used analog drawing with playwrights to help them find the essence of a character, scene, or emotional state. For example, a writer may be working on a character who is severely depressed, but the depiction of that depression seems flat, lifeless, and dull, rather like the actual experience of depression. The dilemma is how to lift the level of language and imagery and crystallize the feeling in a way that is fresh and compelling, without losing the essential nature of the depression itself. Instead of having them reach for a thesaurus that will give a rather predictable list of synonyms, I encourage my students to reach for a pencil and a sketchpad. Perhaps this depression is both comforting and torturous in the same moment; perhaps the character cherishes and despises the soft, gray deadness that envelops him. What is the shape of depression? As they draw what they cannot express entirely in words, they come to know the concept in an entirely new way.

According to Edwards, analog drawings consist of lines—fast and slow, broken or flowing, heavy or light, straight or curving—and of the shapes that are formed as lines are combined. What is most important about the drawing is the feeling state that it captures. The strength of the lines, their hardness or softness, indicates the intensity of feeling. The direction of the lines on the page, whether they press down or flow upward, communicates suppression or release. Shapes placed at the bottom of the page bear the weight of the negative space above, while shapes at the top of the page float above the negative space below. Lines that reach upward have velocity, energy, and release. Sharp little lines in a staccato pattern have an inherent tempo and rhythm. Tensional forces within the drawings manifest themselves as changes of direction, flow, and energy. Analogs give objective existence to subjective states of being. In an analog drawing, form and content are one. Like music, their messages defy cultural barriers and can be understood in many languages. Thought becomes visible. Structure is meaning.[7]

The exercises that follow are designed to provide physical and visual pathways to your own psychophysical space. We hope that by experiencing balance in your body, you will be able to sense the difference between a physical state that is aligned, in that the tensional forces are omnidirectional, and a posture that is comfortable simply because it is habitual. A greater sensitivity to your own feelings of balance and imbalance may translate to a felt sense of these forces within your characters or in the development of action in your plot. Exercises in analog drawing may provide tools to help you see what you feel. The full activation of our psychophysical selves can expand our vocabularies into the domains of both mind and body.

MOVEMENT: THE FORM

Many years ago, in his eternal search for different approaches to teaching movement for actors, Jim explored alignment issues through the Alexander Technique and Feldenkrais' Awareness Through Movement. He also used elements of the martial art aikido to work on balance and centering. All of these different techniques served well enough to help actors find a greater ease and economy of motion and to rid them of their habitual idiosyncrasies, but Jim continued to look for a more active approach with greater emphasis on gross movement components. At a workshop he attended in Los Angeles, Jim found exactly what he was looking for in a system called the Form, a technique originated by Michael Nebadon, a former dancer and teacher of the biomechanical nature of balance.[8] The Form is more than just another set of exercises; it is a way of "being in the body" that can be used in conjunction with other body disciplines and applied to sports and exercise. This movement work is as applicable to writers as it is to actors, athletes, and dancers.

A key element in understanding the Form is finding a natural state of balance where tensional forces in the body expand omnidirectionally in all six dimensions of up and down, right and left, and forward and back with equal force. According to Nebadon, "this is not a form of body work or massage but an essential balancing which reinstates the natural flow of energy, giving the student a totally new experience of the lightness, connection and suspended nature of the physical body in balance. This new experience prompts the release of all forms of stress, discomfort and pain."[9]

For writers who sit in more or less fixed positions for hours at a time, balance is a crucial concept. Whether you are consciously aware of it or not, the physical balance you find in sitting affects the flow of energy and ideas between mind and body. Common habits that can result in imbalance are slumping in the chair, sitting more onto one hip than the other (often caused by crossing the legs), tensing or hunching the shoulders, and thrusting the neck forward to stare at the computer screen or keyboard. Eventually the imbalance will cause fatigue, stress, and even physical pain because the tensional relationships within the body are out of alignment. Relief can be found by restoring the balance either through taking short breaks to actually practice the Form or, even better, by finding a way to integrate the Form into your natural way of sitting.

In the following pages you will find a series of exercises that will allow you to find this state of balance in your own body. But first it is essential to understand how omnidirectional tensional force works to provide this essential balancing. Consider the human body in space.

In order to experience a state of balance, three polarizations must occur at once: above and below, front and back, right and left. A sense of equal force is experienced from all six directions at once. (See Figure 3–1.)

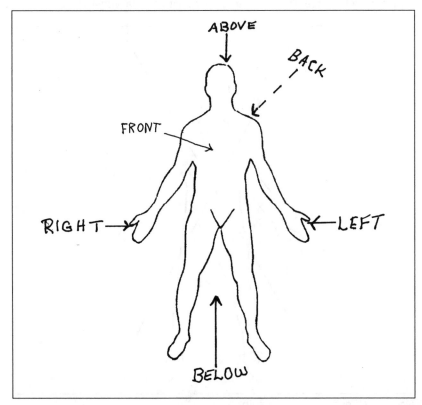

Figure 3–1. Polarities

Imagine a vector extending from the left shoulder, through the center of the body, and out through the right thigh joint. Now pass a second vector from the right shoulder, through the center of the body, and out through the left thigh joint. This illustrates the tensional relationships that exist between these body parts. (See Figure 3–2.)

Now imagine another vector that passes from the sternum, through the center of the body, and out through the coccyx or sacral area. The intersection of all of these vectors is the midline of the body. Now send a final vector from the seventh cervical in the neck, through the center of the body, and out through the abdominal/pubic area. (See Figure 3–3.)

If you extend these lines beyond the body and into space and then connect the points, you get a perfect sphere. (See Figure 3–4, p. 52.)

When the body is in balance, the interior and exterior lines are in alignment; the vertical and horizontal forces are united and not in opposition. The head and pelvic girdle are united and the vertebrae are centered vertically and horizontally in space. The spine is free within its natural curvature.

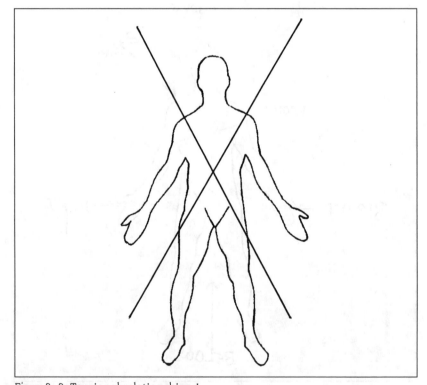

Figure 3–2. Tensional relationships 1

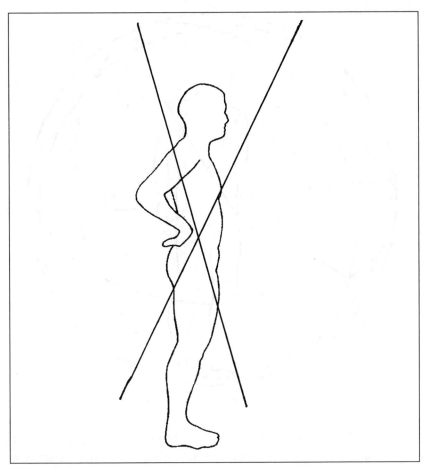

Figure 3–3. Tensional relationships 2

When the body is unbalanced, the result is skeletal and muscular abuse, resulting in excessive tension, compression, and restriction. For example, if the chest is thrust forward, or the pelvis is tipped back, the vertical and horizontal forces are no longer united; they become oppositional. Gravity works against the body's natural balance and movement is restricted. If one hip is out of alignment, the entire symmetry of the diagonal vector is thrown out of kilter and skeletal stress results.

The relationship of muscle tissue and skeletal bones is of vital importance to ease and flow of movement. If there is restriction, or a lack of mobility, it is not due to any one part, but to the relationship that exists within the whole body moving together. Many people are never out of pain because they are

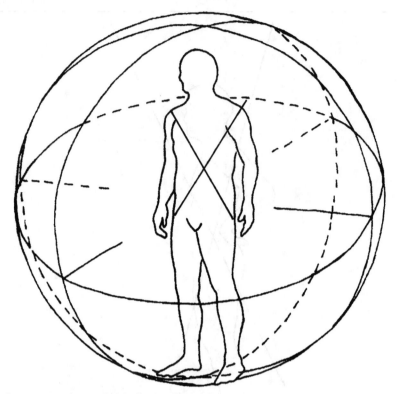

Figure 3–4. Sphere of Balanced Relationships

never in balance. Much of the pain caused by imbalance may be held sub-
consciously and manifest itself in a general feeling of "dis-ease," which is so
subtle that we have come to regard it as simply the way we usually feel.

Sometimes we think of balance as a static form of postural alignment.
Standing up straight, forcing the spine into a rigid position, pulling the
shoulders back, tightening the neck muscles, and keeping the head still
enough to balance a bible may work for the military at attention! But this
isn't balance; it's tension, and tension begets more tension. Rigidity is
counterproductive in movement and in thought. By increasing your sensitivity to true balance within the body, you will find some relief from the
stress caused by hours of sitting, but, on a deeper level, you will also find
greater clarity of thought, emotional availability, and a keener sense of your
own sensory awareness.

In the following pages you will find a series of exercises that will help provide a muscular understanding of the Form, but it is difficult to truly experi-

ence this approach by simply reading about it. It is far preferable to have an instructor or leader help you work through the exercises. With this limitation in mind, we have written these activities to be reminders of the way your body naturally moves when it achieves what Nebadon now calls "Essential Balancing through Unity in Motion."

The Form: Exercises

Experiencing the Sphere

Stand in a comfortable position and hold your arms out in front of you, making a sphere with the inside circle of your arms, keeping a distance between your fingertips.

Release the elbows out, extending and lengthening from the shoulders out.

Move the arms up and down several times while in this spherical relationship.

Gradually, increase the movement, moving the arms above the head and down to the hips.

When you bring the arms up above your head, keep them in the sphere; your rib cage will release down. This improves breathing and releases holding patterns in the rib cage. (This movement is different from the typical instruction to place the arms straight above the head, which causes the rib cage to thrust forward and restricts breathing.)

Just to feel the difference, try lifting the arms straight up.

Notice the tightness between the shoulders and the more restricted breath.

To discover how efficient and balanced this movement is, place your arms in the sphere in front of the body and drop one elbow, then turn the head from side to side.

You will feel a restriction and inhibition of the neck on the side where the elbow is dropped.

Merely by bringing your elbow back up into the sphere shape and repeating the neck movement, you will find that the neck muscles will be free and the connection between the shoulder, arm, and neck will be more dynamic.

Make breath a conscious choice when doing all of these exercises.

Head and Neck

When done properly, these movements will exercise every major muscle in the neck, without the vertebral stress and compression that often result from typical head rolls.

Up and Down

Start with the Form (the sphere) and let your head follow the direction of your arms.

Lift the arms up toward the ceiling and down toward the floor.

As your arms move down, your head follows, chin toward the sternum.

When the arms go toward the ceiling, your face goes toward the ceiling. Take care to lengthen your neck rather than collapse it back and down.

Repeat this several times; then you can move your arms and head in opposition, that is, arms up, head down, and vice versa.

Side to Side

Move your head (ear in line with your shoulder) to one side and bring the opposite arm up and down, still in its spherical shape.

Move the arm down and out to the side or in front of the body, still keeping the sphere. After exploring all of the possible positions, find the one that feels as if it could use more ease and abide in that position for a few seconds longer.

Now move to the other side and execute the same motions.

You will experience this in your trapezius and across the top of the shoulders.

This can be done while sitting or standing. It's a great, easy way to release tension while sitting at your desk.

Diagonals

Move your head diagonally forward to the left (and to the right when repeating), and move the arm on the opposite side up and down, in and out, in its spherical shape.

Move your head diagonally back to the left (and to the right when repeating), and move the opposite arm up and down, in and out, while in its spherical shape.

The arm always goes no further back than the midline of the body; it is, in fact, slightly forward. Always keep the shape of the sphere; otherwise you pull against yourself and disrupt the tensional relationship and balance.

Lower Body

Knees

Hold your arms in the Form in front of your body and lift one knee.

Move your arms up as you raise your knee, and release them down when the knee returns to a standing position.

Keep the shape even when releasing the arms down.

Repeat with the other knee.

It might be helpful to imagine a line attached to the sternum with the other end connected to the top of the knee.

If you feel yourself wobbling, just breathe into the motion.

Repeat this movement several times.

Integration of Upper and Lower Body

Face front with your legs in a wider stance than normal and your arms in the Form.

Bend the knees and shift to the right, which fully straightens the left leg. Reach up with the right arm while keeping the left arm in front.

Keep both arms in a spherical dimension and the torso facing front.

Move back to center, bringing the arms front and once again bending the knees.

Repeat the movement on the left side.

When you are fully extending to one side, the toes on the opposite foot will be touching the floor.

Eventually, you can work up to bringing this foot off the floor. This will get the hip involved.

Repeat this entire sequence three or four times.

Floor Work

Lying Down

Get into a prone position with your knees pulled up toward the ceiling and your feet on the floor.

Place your arms above your chest in the Form.

Work your arms slowly down toward the hips and then up toward the head.

Repeat this movement several times before reaching the full extension of the arms to the floor above your head and down opposite your hips.

These movements may be done while alternating the arms, that is, with one arm going up while the other moves down.

Explore these up-and-down movements with arms always in the sphere, making the circumference of the sphere larger or smaller by holding your arms more widely apart or bringing them together. Always keep the sphere!

You will become aware of where you need to work as you experience twinges of tension.

Remember, you want to lengthen your muscles rather than shorten them. Always take the pressure off your joints.

Don't abuse your bones!

Sitting

Sit up and cross your legs (tailor position).

Using the Form, reach forward and up, then back to center.

Keep your sit bones in contact with the floor as you reach.

Always check to be sure that you are keeping the sphere and try to avoid collapsing down as you reach forward.

Keep your spine lengthened.

Walking, Running, Leaping

Put your arms in the Form and start walking.

Allow your body to follow where your arms lead.

Keep your arms in the Form, opening up the sphere as you move.

Allow the arms to move in opposition up and down.

Avoid allowing the released arm to move back beyond the body's midline. Keep both arms in the sphere.

The leading arm is, in reality, leading your energy; all you must do is follow it.

Walk a little faster and faster, still keeping the arms in the Form.

Try running and leaping.

Remember to always keep the arms leading the body, and follow that energy.

Run faster!

Leap higher!

Soar!

This is fun!

Using the Form in Exercise and Sports

Once you have experienced the sphere of the Form, try using it with other kinds of exercise. As you work out with weight machines, consciously widen your arms and see how much less effort you will expend. Try swimming with the Form, holding the sphere as you stroke the water. You will be amazed at how much more ease and stamina you will discover.

PSYCHOPHYSICAL SPACE EXERCISES

Analog Drawings Exercise 1: Feelings

It is helpful to first experience analog drawing with broad concepts such as emotional states before attempting a more subtle application such as drawing analogs of characters and thematic elements. This exercise has been taken directly from Betty Edwards' *Drawing on the Artist Within*.

Drawing

Label each of five pieces of paper with one of the following words:

1. anger
2. joy
3. fear
4. depression
5. confidence

Read each word to yourself several times.

Allow the feeling state to inhabit your body, your arm, your hand, and your fingers and allow the drawing to come out of your feeling.

Do not try to visualize what the drawing will look like.
Using a pencil, draw an analog response to each of the words under the label.

Use only the language of line and abstract shapes and forms.

Do not use any pictorial symbols of any kind.

Do not include any words.

Make a different drawing for each emotional state.

Reading the Drawings

Once you have completed all five analog drawings, they can now be read, not for what they look like artistically, but for what they tell you about the feeling, concept, or character you are exploring. Every element becomes a visual metaphor. In the act of reading, the drawing teaches you its meaning.

Look for similarities and differences within your own drawings.

How do they handle space?

Are there similarities of kinds of lines?

Are there similarities in the placement within the square?

How are drawings different from each other?

Attend to the tensional qualities in the drawings.

Are lines and shapes in opposition to each other?

Is there harmony between lines and shapes?

Look for vectors of energy (strong diagonal lines).

Look for lines and shapes that interrupt the flow of energy.

Which drawings are more or less powerful for you?

Drawings into Words

Select two drawings that are particularly powerful for you. Use words to tag the drawings by finishing the following sentences. Replace (*anger*) with whatever feeling you have chosen.

This (anger) is . . .

This (anger) feels . . .

This (anger) moves . . .

This (anger) wants . . .

Once you have tagged both drawings by finishing the sentences for each, select the one that is particularly powerful for you.

Cluster the word.

Using both the cluster and the tag sentences as inspiration, write a vignette.

The vignette may be in any form—poetry, dialogue, character study, narrative, and so on.

Creating an Analog Museum

If you are doing this exercise in a class or workshop, it can be interesting to compare and contrast the drawings of participants. Place all the selected drawings based upon the same word together in a group, so that there are five groups of drawings in various places in the room. Invite all of the participants to visit each group of drawings.

Look for similarities between drawings of the same word.

Look for differences between drawings of the same word.

Invite volunteers to their read vignettes.

Encourage the group to try to guess which vignette came from which drawing.

Analog Drawings Exercise 2: Characters

Divide a single sheet of paper into four equal parts and label each with the name of a character in a single play you are working on. Be sure all characters are from the same play.

Drawing

Read the character's name to yourself several times.

Allow an image of a specific scene or key moment for that character to be conjured in your mind.

Try to think of a moment when the tensional forces within that character are particularly intense.

Do not try to visualize what the drawing will look like.

Using a pencil, draw an analog response to the character.

Use only the language of line.

Do not use any pictorial symbols of any kind.

Do not include any words.

Do this for each of the four characters.

Reading the Drawings

Look for similarities and differences among your own drawings.

> Do certain characters seem better defined to you than other characters?

> Are these characters primary or secondary?

> Sometimes minor characters are etched with greater clarity than major ones.

Might this analog change if you had conjured a different moment in the play?

Attend to the tensional qualities in the drawings.

How are these tensional forces revealed in the character's behavior?

How are these tensional qualities reflected in the character's speech?

> Tempo, rhythm, and pace?

> Word choice?

> Length of line?

Drawings into Words

Use words to tag the character drawings by finishing the following sentences.

Replace (*this character*) with the character's name.

> (This character) moves . . .

> (This character) wants . . .

> (This character) needs . . .

(This character) feels . . .

(This character) fears . . .

(This character) hopes . . .

(This character) dreams . . .

Scene Work

Write a brief scene that would *never* happen in the actual play, where all four of these characters interact in some way.

Attend to the tensional forces that exist within and between characters.

Characters need not belong to the same time period or frame of reality; that is, characters can appear in dreams, flashbacks, or as interior voices.

The scene need not, indeed should not, be part of the present play.

Allow the scene to evolve from the tensional forces between characters.

The purpose of this exercise is to explore characters, their tensional forces, and their relationships and not to generate new scene material for the play. Only if you are totally free from the self-imposed responsibility that the scene has to work are you really free to explore what else could happen. The characters are here to teach you about who they are, what they want, what they are afraid of, and what they dream about. Allow them to inform you!

Character and Theme Collages

A character collage is a form of visual metaphor and self-discovery. In this activity you will create a three-dimensional piece made up of found objects, images, pictures, and so on. Attend to all sensory information, not just visual. Some pieces may be included because of their texture, smell, or even taste.

Character Sculptures

Take several days to allow objects and elements to choose you.

Trust your instinct and intuition as you select elements.

Allow the character to define him or herself through the objects. Don't impose your own assumptions on how the sculpture should look.

Use all of your senses, not just the visual.

Arrangement

Allow the size and shape of the sculpture to be determined by the character.

Pieces may be as simple or complex as they need to be to express the essence of the character.

Writing from the Sculpture

Once the sculpture is assembled and feels right, write a brief monologue in which the sculpture describes itself to you.

The sculpture is doing the talking, *not* the character, *not* you!

Allow the sculpture to tell you about aspects of the character that you do not know yet.

Theme Collage

Make a three-dimensional collage that expresses the themes, motifs, and questions explored in your play. Pay particular attention to size and scale, color and texture, images and shapes. The collage may be any size that is appropriate for the piece; it may have an inside and an outside, moving parts, light and shadow, or even a sound accompaniment. Allow the arrangement of elements to serve as a metaphor for the piece. Allow this collage to tell you things about your play that you do not already know.

A WORD OR TWO . . .

I have used analog drawings, character sculptures, and theme collages in almost every playwriting class I have ever taught, and many of my students have found them to be among the most useful activities they have ever done. Working from abstraction encourages right-brain thinking and helps writers make an emotional connection with their material in ways that surpass the normal intellectual processes. Some students, however, have been a bit wary of this rather unorthodox approach, fearing that they can't draw or paint or that they have no art training. Once they discover that these activities aren't about art, they are about discovery, they relax and enjoy working on their plays in such a different way. One student eventually found a path to the heart of her play when she created an enormous collage on the box for her queen-sized futon. The play was a retelling of the Greek myth of Medea.[10] There was something about the size of the box that was liberating and perfectly in keeping with the monumental scale of her story and characters. Another student, working on a play titled *theevolutionofwoman*, built a character sculpture entirely out of household products, with a string mop for hair, sponges, and rubber gloves. This collection of everyday items perfectly captured the tone of irony and paradox that she was trying to achieve.[11]

In the exploration of psychophysical space, we receive information in kinesthetic experience and in visual images. Just as the Form can bring greater ease to a writer's body in the arduous task of sitting still, it can also open the mind to a deeper understanding of tensional forces. All of these techniques are simply ways of helping us discover what our bodies and minds have to teach us.

NOTES

1. Yi-Fu Tuan, *Space and Place: The Perspective of Experience* (Minneapolis: University of Minnesota Press, 1977).

2. Ibid., 43.

3. Paul Castagno, *New Playwriting Strategies: A Language-Based Approach to Playwriting* (New York: Routledge, 2001), 12.

4. Ibid.

5. Andrea Moon, *Weight* (master's thesis play, University of Texas at Austin, 2001).

6. Betty Edwards, *Drawing on the Artist Within* (New York: Simon and Schuster, 1986), 66–95.

7. Ibid.

8. Further information about Michael Nebadon can be found on the following website: www.speaking.com/speakers/michaelcristiamnebadon.html.

9. Michael Nebadon, "Essential Balancing Through Unity in Motion," Speakers Platform, www.speaking.com/speakers/michaelcristiamnebadon.html.

10. Carlia Francis, *Twilight's Ending* (master's thesis play, University of Texas at Austin, 1998).

11. Lucia Del Vecchio, *theevolutionofwoman* (master's thesis play, University of Texas at Austin, 2002).

4
CHAPTER

Interpersonal Space

IN THIS CHAPTER WE WILL EXPLORE THE SPACE THAT EXISTS BETWEEN and among people and groups. In our previous explorations of child and psychophysical spaces, we were primarily concerned with the internal states that exist within and help us define and create a sense of self. In this chapter, however, we shall look to the external bonds and boundaries, the territories and taboos that deepen an understanding of self in relation to other people. Interpersonal space is created in the complex webs of personal and professional, intimate and distant, casual and long-lasting relationships that we weave between ourselves and others.

As playwrights, we create interpersonal space in many ways: in the tensional forces that exist between characters, in the patterns of their verbal and nonverbal communication, and in the ever changing dynamics of relationships that evolve throughout the course of the play. No character is ever an entity unto him- or herself. Even in a solo performance, a single actor often embodies multiple characters, changing identities with subtle variations of vocal tone, body language, or costume pieces. Dramatic action usually involves at least two or more characters creating or resolving conflict. The dramatic action of a play or performance piece consists largely of these fluid, ever changing interactions.

In linear, plot-centered plays, interactions between characters tend to be based on cause and effect. One character says or does something to another character that brings about a change in their relationship. In more abstract, experimental pieces, interactions may have connections other than linear logic and might be expressed in movement patterns, visual images, or ideas expressed verbally and physically. In all live performances, a form of interpersonal space is created between performers and members of the audience. Usually, this is a place where spectators are invited to identify or empathize with characters. Sometimes, however, the space is deliberately aggressive and confrontational, as in the agitprop pieces created by political theatre companies in the 1960s and '70s, in which the purpose was to distance or affront the audience.

SPACE AND OTHERS

In a very real sense, our perception of the size and comfort of a particular space is determined by who else shares it with us. Our awareness of spaciousness and crowding is not really conditioned by the size of a particular area, but by how and by whom it is filled. In nature, even if an area is crowded, it can still seem spacious. Being alone in a forest gives you the feeling of vastness, solitude, and peace. But the forest is actually very crowded with trees, branches, and bushes. It is anything but quiet. As I write this I am sitting in my outdoor "office" in the middle of a forest of ponderosa pine. In the distance I hear the wind approaching with the force of a far-away freight train; the breeze in the scrub oak rustles; grasshoppers clatter; hummingbirds whirr; bees buzz; crows caw back and forth in a cacophony of sound. This is a very noisy place, but I experience it as peaceful, quiet, and spacious. Suddenly, the telephone rings. The presence of one other person on the other end of the line causes the forest to disappear, and the world shrinks into the earpiece of the receiver.

Geographer Yi-Fu Tuan suggests that it is people rather than objects, things, or sounds that restrict our space. It is not the number of people, but the interpersonal relationships we have with them that expand or contract our experience of our own personal space. On a bustling New York City street, we can feel quite alone in our anonymity, but we can feel crowded in a large empty space if it is shared by even one other person. Imagine practicing a piano in a darkened, empty theatre. In the safety of your solitude, you play magnificently; your imagination launches you into the infinite spaciousness of the music. A cough from the darkness betrays the presence of a listener, and the space contracts to an uncomfortable closeness.

The theatrical spaces we create as playwrights will be spacious or crowded depending on the interactions between characters and their environments.

The feeling of vastness of the blasted plain where Didi and Gogol wait for Godot is a result of their intimacy with each other in contrast to their isolation from the rest of the world. Even in a tiny theatre, the space surrounding these two characters seems enormous. Compare this to the claustrophobia of Sartre's *No Exit*, where three characters in a closed room discover that Hell is, indeed, "other people."

TERRITORIES

Interpersonal space is intimately connected to how we create and defend territories. We can invite other beings to share our personal space, or we can keep them out verbally, physically, and emotionally. In *People Space: The Making and Breaking of Human Boundaries*, anthropologist Norman Ashcraft and psychiatrist Albert Scheflen present a fascinating analysis of the various ways people shape, share, and defend personal space. "Man is a territorial animal very much like his fellow creatures. He defines space and marks it out for his particular use. He draws visible and invisible boundaries which he expects others to respect. He will defend a territory against the intrusion of others."[1] A territory may be a tract of land, a nation, a community, your own backyard, or an intangible space such as a privileged relationship or an emotional state. A marriage is a kind of territory that two people enter with the expectation of certain rights of intimacy and responsibilities of fidelity. A job may be a territory, where one person fiercely defends his or her turf against possible usurpers. Even an intangible psychological state such as depression may feel like a bleak and lonely landscape. Any outsider attempting to enter these territories, for good or ill, must cross barriers of law, custom, consciousness, or behavior.

In plays, territories are not just physical and geographical; they are also emotional, political, philosophical, and even spiritual. In Edward Albee's *Zoo Story*, Peter and Jerry battle over a park bench with deadly consequences. In Tony Kushner's *Homebody/Kabul*, territories are both political and familial, as he brings Afghan cultural taboos into conflict with the dysfunctional dynamics of a middle-class English family. In some plays, characters serve as territories of refuge for other characters. In Tennessee Williams' *The Night of the Iguana*, Hannah, a middle-aged spinster, says to the cynical, dissipated Shannon:

> We make a home for each other, my Grandfather and I. . . . I don't mean what other people mean when they speak of a home, because I don't regard a home as a . . . well, a place, a building . . . a house . . . of wood, bricks, stone. I think of a home as being a thing that two people have between them in which they can . . . well, nest—rest—live in, emotionally speaking.[2]

Relationship as refuge is in sharp contrast to relationship as battleground, as seen in the torturous territory of George and Martha's marriage in Edward Albee's *Who's Afraid of Virginia Woolf?* Nick and Honey are invited back to George and Martha's house after a faculty party, and what begins as an innocent round of after-dinner drinks escalates into a free-for-all where all territories of professional, personal, and sexual propriety are invaded and crossed, time and time again. Sometimes a territory is most powerful when a character feels excluded and longs for entry. In Carson McCuller's play and novel *The Member of the Wedding*, twelve-year-old Frankie yearns for an emotional space where she truly belongs.

> The trouble with me is that for a long time I have been just an "I" person. All other people can say "we." When Bernice says "we" she means her lodge and church and colored people. Soldiers can say "we" and mean the army. All people belong to a "we" except me. . . . Not to belong to a "we" makes you too lonesome. . . . I know the bride and my brother are the "we" of me.[3]

BOUNDARIES

Humans and animals mark territories in various ways. In the wild, deer bite the bark of trees around the perimeter of their feeding ground to warn others away. Coyotes and mountain lions mark their hunting grounds with their urine and feces, as do wolves. A bull elk uses a boundary of sound to mark his territory with his own distinctive bugle call. Most territorial marking in nature has to do with survival issues of hunting and mating. Humans are more diverse in their strategies for marking territories, using everything from weapons of mass destruction to body language to delineate and defend their space. In "civilized" societies, behavioral codes, laws, contracts, manners, and mutual agreements are the primary ways people set boundaries.

Many plays have at their core issues of creating and crossing borders. In the same way that virtually all dramatic action moves from balance to imbalance, many plays and performance events involve characters who try to invade or cross some kind of border and are met with opposition by those who defend it. Sometimes it is a physical turf. The Sharks and Jets of *West Side Story* use fists and knives to protect their patches of asphalt, just as the Montagues and Capulets used swords centuries before. Sometimes the boundary is one of sexual propriety. In Harold Pinter's *The Homecoming*, Lenny brings his bride, Ruth, to meet his father and brothers. She seduces the men and takes possession of their home. In Paula Vogel's *How I Learned to Drive*, Uncle Peck crosses every border of trust and intimacy in his sexual abuse of his niece, Li'l Bit. Nontraditional plays are also filled with examples of invasions of one kind of space by foragers from another. The characters in Caryl Churchill's *Cloud Nine* trespass over boundary lines of time, place, gender, and identity, seemingly at will. Each time a border is crossed, both territories are illuminated.

INVASION AND DEFENSE

In theatre, as in life, predators recognize borders and territories and make a conscious choice to violate them. Some incursions are more overt than others. At one extreme are the violent encounters of warfare, street crimes, and physical combat; at the opposite end, the chill of silence and exclusion can be equally, but differently, devastating. Behind each of these encounters, from geopolitical warfare to the slap of domestic abuse, a border has been set and violated, a territory defended and lost. When a predator invades a territory or crosses a clearly marked boundary, it is usually not by accident. The aggressor comes with malice or mischief in mind.

As writers, we often try to place our characters in as much physical, emotional, and ethical jeopardy as possible. Tensional forces in the interpersonal relationships between characters are the battlegrounds where psychological and ethical issues are played out in action. Since the time of the Greeks, violent behavior between human beings has been the galvanizing force of dramatic action. Violence may be the overt issue of the play, manifested in the inciting incident, the climax, and the denouement, or it may serve as the cultural background of the environment. But without sufficient attention to development of character, the inevitability of action, and the consequences of choice, violence loses its impact and becomes gratuitous. It is just another thing that happens. When violence seems excessive, it is usually because it has been used as a plot point to be exploited rather than an ethical issue to be explored or a dimension of character. The writer has been concerned primarily with the violent event itself and has paid less attention to the path that preceded it or to the implications of its aftermath.

Thankfully, interpersonal space is not solely made up of tensional relationships and violent behavior. The subtle, or not so subtle, signs that remove barriers and allow borders to be crossed are also important. Scenes of recognition and reconciliation, declarations of hidden feelings, and the healing of old hurts allow characters to welcome each other into deeply personal territories. Sometimes these scenes are hard to write without becoming mired in sentimentality. Conflict almost always leads to action, but resolution requires subtlety. It is often helpful to look to the obstacles that prevent a character from declaring his or her true feelings or to explore nonverbal choices of gesture and body language that reveal, rather than declare, that character's intentions. A glance, a touch, a hand extended, but not yet taken may be far more articulate than words. It is often the aching space left by words that remain unspoken that is the most eloquent.

SPACE AND BEHAVIOR

On both large and small scales, our concepts of interpersonal space are also determined by culture and are reflected in social codes of behavior. Some cultures are more comfortable with proximity and physical touch than others. According to Ashcraft and Scheflen, when members of a highly tactile cultural tradition touch people of a nontactile tradition, discomfort, embarrassment, or even violent behavior may result. "The buffer zone between two Cubans casually conversing . . . may be as small as eighteen inches. The same space under the same conditions between two Englishmen will exceed a yard."[4] Behind the cultural stereotypes of the backslapping Uncle Luigi or the bear-hug-giving Cousin Nykos or the stiff upper everything of prim Miss Prism, there are very real cultural spatial differences.

For the writer, the pitfall here is to exaggerate this overt behavior to such an extent that the character becomes a hollow stereotype. We have only to look at television sitcoms to see this in action: *All* Greeks are loud, overbearing, and hug each other all the time. *All* Jewish mothers cling to their sons and hate their daughters-in-law. *All* Englishwomen are reserved and distant. While it is true that there are distinct cultural similarities in the ways different people create and maintain their interpersonal space, these patterns are not the *only* defining characteristics in their repertoire of behavior. Also, there are often exceptions within cultures, where individuals contradict the stereotypes identified with their heritage. An insightful playwright will build on the foundation of these spatial generalizations to create fully developed characters by contrasting specifics and by clearly defining patterns of interaction.

PATTERNS OF COMMUNICATION

Communication patterns are the building blocks of interpersonal space. It is not only the content of what we say and do that establishes a relationship with another person but also how we send messages and how others receive them. Communication patterns may be sent and received visually in signs, symbols, images, and pictures; transmitted through words and sound in tone of voice, pitch, tempo, and volume; or expressed physically in facial expressions, body language, gesture, and movement. These are the primary vocabularies of expression among humans: verbal, visual, and kinesthetic. They are also the primary languages of the stage. At any given moment on stage, a performance communicates in at least two and usually all three of these languages simultaneously: in words and sounds, images and pictures, and movement and gestures.

In the early 1970s, John Grindler, a professor of linguistics, and psychologist Richard Bandler developed a system to model structures of effective thinking and communication between individuals. They gave their model the tongue-twisting name Neuro-Linguistic-Programming, or NLP. Today this system is used in psychology to assist therapist-client communication, in business to enhance marketing strategies, and in education to assist teacher-student interaction. According to the theories of NLP, people receive and send messages most effectively in one of three primary representational systems: verbal, visual, or kinesthetic.[5] Although these systems are not mutually exclusive, each person has a primary or preferred modality that is reflected in speech patterns, verbal and visual metaphors, and the habitual language he or she uses to reflect or represent experience. Put simply, most people receive information and express themselves most effectively in one of these three modes: words and sounds, images and pictures, or feelings and movement. Although this is a gross oversimplification of a complex and fascinating body of theory, the whole notion of representation systems is useful to playwrights in a number of ways.

Think of your own writing for a moment. When you are creating a scene in your imagination, do you tend to see the action first? Does the idea come to you in a series of visual impressions, colors, shapes, still or moving photographs that present themselves to the eye of your mind? Or do you hear words and sounds? Do you hear voices speaking dialogue, singing songs, or simply tones, harmonies, and melodies? Perhaps you access the feeling state first in the emotional dynamics of a scene: the heat of the anger in an argument, the sexual arousal of a flirtation, the cool precision of a logical explanation. As you write, all of your sensory channels will eventually come into play, but chances are that your initial impulse will originate in the same sensory modality that you use to perceive and store your own experience of the world.

Knowledge of the representation systems can also be useful in looking at the way characters express themselves and communicate with each other. In Tennessee Williams' A *Streetcar Named Desire*, Blanche Dubois displays all the signs of a visual representation system. She is desperately concerned with appearances; she covers bare light bulbs with paper lanterns. Her memories and stories are a series of pictures in which she replays her past as a fanta-sized movie of her life. Although Blanche is extremely verbal and uses lan-guage as both a seduction and a defense, the imagery of her speech is highly visual. Stanley, on the other hand, is emphatically kinesthetic. His body is the locus of his thought; his physical and emotional needs control his actions. He distrusts words and "painting fancy pictures" and trusts only action and behavior. The highly charged chemistry that exists between Blanche and Stanley is partially the result of the tension created by the differences of their representational systems, but it is also fueled by gut-level attraction. Stanley intuitively senses that deeply buried under the visual fantasies and verbal ex-cesses that Blanche uses as a smoke screen is a smoldering kinesthetic soul mate with a sexual appetite as great or greater than his own.

It might be interesting to go through your own work and disregard, just for the moment, the content of what your characters say to each other, and look to the kinds of verbal patterns they use. Is there a dominant representational system apparent in the ways they interact? Look to your use of imagery. Is there a pattern here? How does your own primary representational system af-fect those of your characters? Might you find more variety and specificity in the voices of your characters by consciously manipulating the representa-tional systems they use?

We sometimes assume that the words of our characters are their primary mode of communication. But this isn't always true. As playwrights, we cannot depend on the slender meanings of words alone to carry the weight of com-munication. It is often the nonverbal dynamics that exist between characters, the silent arguments and the wordless reconciliations, that are the most ef-fective. In Oscar Wilde's *The Importance of Being Ernest*, Cecily and Gwendolyn treat each other with elaborate politeness, but their true feelings contradict their honeyed words. This meaning behind the meaning is called the subtext. The interpersonal space between two characters is often most articulately rendered in a reversed code of meanings and intentions where words say one thing and bodies say something quite different. The tensional relationship between text and subtext, between words and actions, creates a momentum that propels the action forward.

Sometimes in plays, as in life, the interpersonal space that exists between two or more people can be fraught with tension or as easy as a gently flowing stream. Relationships are expressed in words and actions, sounds and silences, and can be so emotionally charged that they almost seem to be characters in themselves. In Albee's Who's Afraid of Virginia Woolf? both George and Martha are distinct and individual characters, but the relationship that crackles between them is so monstrous and powerful that it has an identity of its own; it is almost palpable.

In the movement discussion and the writing exercises that follow, we will find ways to explore and represent interpersonal space with bodies, words, and visual images.

MOVEMENT: CONTACT IMPROVISATION

Contact improvisation is, perhaps, the quintessential movement form in which to explore interpersonal space. It is often referred to as a physical conversation between two or more people. In its duet form, two people move together in contact, maintaining a spontaneous physical dialogue through kinesthetic signals. There are no preset exercises or patterns of movement. Both individuals move together, mutually bearing, sharing, releasing, and supporting each other's weight through a series of shifting points of contact between their two bodies. Contact may be hand to hand, hip to shoulder, back to front, or foot to knee as the center of movement and interaction constantly shifts and changes. All movements are improvised, created spontaneously, as each partner responds to the touch of the other and initiates movement in an unbroken flow. In contact improvisation, each person experiences the territory of his or her own body most fully by inviting at least one other person to cross the boundary of touch and to create movement together.

In a group, contact improvisation is an ensemble activity. Sessions, usually called jams, can become extremely physical as bodies interact with increasing speed and velocity. There is always an element of risk, always an edge of danger. Injuries do happen, but mostly from a lack of attention, focus, or sensitivity to what is actually happening in the physical conversation between bodies. As a performance form, contact improvisation is fascinating to watch as a series of relationships that are initiated and then develop, change, and evolve into new relationships in purely physical terms.[6]

For the writer, contact improvisation can be a tool to open up a wide range of kinesthetic experiences and to deepen an awareness of self, particularly in relationship to the physical presence of others. The intimacy of nonsexual touch requires a different kind of listening, not just with the ears but also with the whole body. Contact improvisation requires that the participant stay fully present in the moment without trying to predetermine what comes next—a valuable lesson for writers. The physicality of the form and the necessity of contact may be threatening to some people, but it can also be exhilarating. The experience of moving in contact with another human being, touch to touch, breath to breath, can be deeply emotional. It simply cannot be adequately described in words; it must be experienced.

Even for writers who do not wish to pursue contact improvisation as a movement form for themselves, an understanding of its principles of physical communication can be useful in clarifying the interactions that take place between characters in their plays. Just as analog drawing allows you to abstract essential qualities and tensional forces, the physical vocabulary of contact improvisation can reveal the essential nature of relationships between characters as they interact and evolve over time. It is possible to abstract these qualities into descriptions of the kinds of interpersonal transactions that might take place in your plays.

In contact improvisation two or more individuals are likely to have

the experience of bearing and giving weight

the experience of coming together and moving apart

the experience of trust in another person for support

the experience of giving support to another person

The physical language of contact improvisation includes the following kinds of interactions:

Torsion: *twisting*	Counterbalance: *sharing*
Traction: *pulling*	Disorientation: *confusion*
Tension: *force*	Spontaneity: *immediacy*
Suspension: *holding*	Safety: *responsibility*
Compression: *pressure*	Contact: *relationship*
Friction: *rubbing*	Balance: *stability*
Gravity: *attraction*	Relaxation: *ease*

Virtually all of these terms can be seen as metaphoric for the interpersonal transactions that take place between characters. For example, in Shakespeare's *Romeo and Juliet*, the Montagues and Capulets are inextricably caught in the *friction* of an ancient feud that *twists* all of their relationships. The Duke of Verona *pressures* both sides to stop fighting by threatening banishment. Romeo and Juliet meet and are immediately *attracted* to one another. Briefly, they find a kind of *balance*; together, they *bear the weight* of each other's love and *mutually support* each other, *trusting* that their love is stronger than the *forces* that *pull them apart* . . . and so on.

Quite a different pattern might emerge if one were to visualize the movement patterns of Lincoln and Booth in Suzan-Lori Parks' Pulitzer Prize-winning *Top Dog/Under Dog*. The title itself can be seen as a kind of contact improvisation between the two brothers, who alternately *support* and *counterbalance* each other and *pull apart*. The "dance" of the play is the changing pattern of their relationship that slowly unravels until one brother finally kills the other.

Many of my students have found their experiences with contact improvisation to be extremely useful in clarifying the kinesthetic dynamics that exist between characters as fluid and ever changing patterns. One student recently combined analog drawing and contact improvisation to produce the chart in Figure 4–1, which chronicles the relationship between two key characters throughout the action of her play.

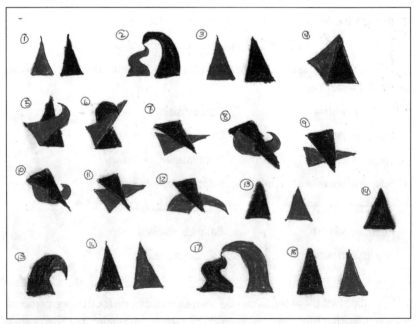

*Figure 4–1. Contact analog

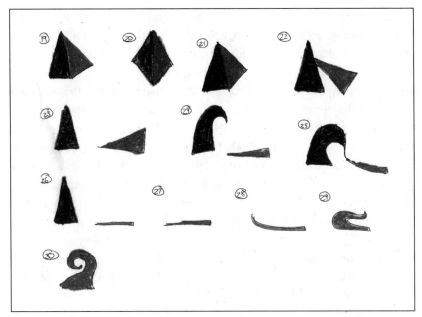

Figure 4–1. Contact analog (cont'd)

Each number refers to a major beat or a scene between the two characters, indicated by the two triangles. First, they stand apart; then they tentatively explore and experiment with different approach and avoidance behaviors. They move together and separate, eventually becoming entwined with each other and ultimately destroying the tentative relationship they had established. When they finally culminate their attraction in sexual union, they destroy their relationship. Gradually the character represented by the triangle on the right recovers and is both stronger and more flexible than before. By representing this "dance" graphically, the playwright was able to see which scenes moved the relationship forward and which kept it static. [7]

Another student in the same class, writing a play about incest, decided to include contact improvisations in specific scenes:

> Sappho looks offstage, concerned. The daughter walks onto the stage, dragging the sheet behind her. The daughter, in a daze, walks past Sappho. As she passes, Sappho picks up the end of the sheet. They begin a contact improvisation, using the sheet as the contact point. This dance should ultimately be about healing. Sappho should "lead" and instruct or help the daughter through the moves of the dance. This contact improvisation should end when the two actors feel that the dance has come to a natural close. Lights fade to dark. [8]

An understanding of contact improvisation can be helpful in the generative phase of a new piece. You may feel the kinesthetic dynamics between characters before you have any idea about the words they might say to each other. Contact improvisation can help you get these notions out of your head and into the physical body. Ask yourself which characters are *attracted* to one another at the beginning of the play. Which characters experience *friction*, or *torsion*, and with whom? How do these physical, psychological, and emotional relationships change over time? What is the wordless dance of your play? You might also enlist the help of a few actor-movers to embody these forces in three dimensions. You might even move them yourself with a willing partner. Once you have experienced your characters in your own muscles and borne their weight on your back, you will know them in quite a different way.

You might also use contact improvisation as a way to help you to look at the themes and issues of your play, particularly if the piece is more about images and ideas as opposed to a linear, naturalistic depiction of character and plot. You might ask yourself what the forces of *torsion* and *tension* are between the ideas at work and how they are made manifest. Do images and ideas *support* each other, or are they deliberately in a state of *friction*? Is the feeling you are trying to engender in your audience one of *stability* or *disorientation* and *confusion*? It is sometimes helpful for playwrights working in abstract forms to explore ways of clarifying their ideas in a way that supports the abstraction. By playing with these concepts in languages other than words, it is possible to clarify what seems vague and unformed in your mind without oversimplification. It is fascinating to consider the dance of images and ideas, particularly in nontraditional plays.

Directors sometimes use contact improvisation as a rehearsal technique to help actors create a physical life for characters and to help them understand and embody the unspoken subtext that may take place between characters. A recent student writing a play with music about a family shattered by pedophilia found that contact improvisation was the perfect way for her to express the physical relationships between characters that were often at odds with their words. Contact improvisation became the choreographic language of the piece even into the final performance.[9]

Whether you use contact improvisation as a generative activity, a rehearsal technique, or a performance form, it is possible to distill the essence of the interpersonal space between characters with great clarity and precision. Like analog drawing, these activities simply expand your vocabulary, even if none of the movement is ever actually used on stage or in the rehearsal room. The more tools you have at your disposal, the more points of access you will find into your own work.

As you move ahead into the exercises, I urge you to be bold and to challenge your own borders and territories and to draw upon physical and visual vocabularies of expression.

INTERPERSONAL SPACE EXERCISES

Explorations of interpersonal space usually involve two or more people in some kind of interaction. Therefore, many of the exercises in this chapter involve some sort of improvisation between two or more participants. In some cases these activities may also easily be done as solo writing experiences.

Territories and Boundaries: **Improvisation (pairs or group)**

Choose a partner and decide between you which of you is A and which is B.

In the following improvisation, A is a boundary maker. Your job is to set as many boundaries as you can, physically, emotionally, and so on. Use any props you wish. Use body language, eye contact. Use verbal ploys, excuses, and so forth. You may *not* use physical force.

A boundary may be a tangible object like the doorway to a room, or a physical action like not allowing anyone to touch anything that belongs to you, not making eye contact, and so on. Once you have set a boundary and you are fairly sure that B understands the boundary, you may choose to either defend or relinquish the boundary in the course of the improvisation.

B is the boundary tester. Your job is to discover as many boundaries as you can and to test them. Remember, *test* is not the same as *smash*; test means test. You may *not* use physical force at any time.

Notice the verbal, visual, and kinesthetic clues of A and use them to your advantage.

Once you have discovered and tested the borders, you may choose to respect them or to invade them.

Possible scenarios for improvisation:

> two passengers flying first-class on a transatlantic flight
>
> the first day on the job for two temp workers
>
> the first day in the dorm of two college roommates

If this activity is done in a workshop or class, have observers try to guess which is A and which is B.

Identify the borders.

Identify the visual, verbal, and kinesthetic strategies for testing and defending borders.

Suggest alternative strategies and replay the scenes.

Territories and Boundaries: Writing

Select a play you have written or one that you are working on that you feel has a clearly defined sense of territories and boundaries.

Create a scene in which one character is a boundary maker and another is a boundary tester.

Use as many different ways of setting and testing boundaries as possible.

verbal

visual

kinesthetic

In this scene a territory should be established and then invaded and then either defended or relinquished without using physical violence of any kind.

Communication Patterns: Movement and Improvisation

Mixed Messages

Stand comfortably in your own space.

Demonstrate the word *no* in your body.

Look at yourself and others.

Some people close off the front of the body by folding arms or crossing legs. Others open the body and stand defiantly. Some people are off-balance or have conflicting balance. Others close their eyes or look away.

Energy often turns inward. Notice what happens with breath; it usually constricts.

Demonstrate the word *yes* in your body and notice the differences.

Many people have a more open stance; their eyes tend to be more open and direct. Their energy moves outward.

Their feet feel lighter and less planted.

Demonstrate *no* with your eyes and *yes* with your body.

    Check out where tension manifests and how it is expressed.

    Which is the stronger message?

Say *no* with the pelvis and *yes* with chest.

    Some people tighten their pelvis and squeeze their buttocks.

    Arms tend to be open and welcoming.

    Which is the stronger message?

Choose a partner and work in pairs.

Designate one of you as A and the other as B.

Using only your bodies in relationship to each other:

    A says, "Here I am."

    B says, "Go away."

See how the messages are made manifest.

Using only your bodies in relationship to each other:

    A says, "Come with me."

    B says, "Leave me alone."

See how the messages are made manifest.

Using only your bodies in relationship to each other:

    A is ambivalent.

    B is purely either *yes* or *no*.

Have a gestural conversation without words and see how A is affected by B's attitude.

Which is stronger—*yes* or *no* or *ambivalence*?

Improvisation with Mixed Messages (improvised or written). Work in pairs.
One person is to have a clearly articulated positive or negative approach to the situation while the other is to continually send mixed messages. Perhaps the body says one thing while words say another. Perhaps one person constantly changes his or her mind or sees alternative points of view.

Which position has greater strength?

Which position has more interest?

How do the interpersonal dynamics between characters change?

Contact Improvisation (*improvised, written, or drawn*)

Select a play you have written or one that you are working on that you feel has a clearly defined progression in the changing patterns of character relationships.

Take a moment or two to jot down a list of sentences that express these dynamics in movement terms. Pay particular attention to the terms used in contact improvisation listed below.

In contact improvisation, two or more individuals are likely to have

the experience of bearing and giving weight

the experience of coming together and moving apart

the experience of trust in another person for support

the experience of giving support to another person

Visualize the dance of the play as a contact improvisation.

Either write or draw this dance in words or symbols.

or

Work with one or more other people to create this dance physically.

Go ahead!
Be brave!
Try this!

A WORD OR TWO . . .

We have not included specific exercises in contact improvisation in this chapter, as it is best to first experience this form in a workshop or jam with other participants led by a sensitive and careful leader. If you have never experienced contact improvisation before, be a bit careful, as it can be physically and emotionally demanding. Contact improvisation often requires people of very different heights, weights, and strengths to share and bear each other's weight. Sometimes movements are extremely slow, but at other times the speed of a slam can be exhilarating and a bit frightening. The physical intimacy of two or more bodies coming together can be extremely powerful. To some it is a vulnerability that makes them uncomfortable; to others it is a deeply moving experience. A sensitive leader will be aware of this and make adjustments accordingly.

Whenever I invite contact improvisation specialists into my class, I always alert them to any students with possible physical or emotional difficulty with direct physical interaction. I always try to structure a writing alternative into any contact improvisation experience so students who wish to can simply sit it out and write their responses to what they see. Sometimes I intentionally ask different participants to step out at various times so this does not become an issue. My students have found contact improvisation to be a very powerful tool in their lives and their work.

NOTES

1. Norman Ashcraft and Albert E. Scheflen, *People Space: The Making and Breaking of Human Boundaries* (New York: Anchor, 1976), 3.

2. Tennessee Williams, *The Night of the Iguana* (New York: New Directions, 1961), 108–9.

3. Carson McCullers, *The Member of the Wedding* (New York: New Directions, 1951), 51–52.

4. Ashcraft and Scheflen, *People Space*, 7.

5. For further information about NLP, see *Introducing Neuro-Linguistic Programming: Psychological Skills for Understanding and Influencing People*, by Joseph O'Connor and John Seymour (London: Element, 2002).

6. For further information about contact improvisation, see *Sharing the Dance: Contact Improvisation and American Culture*, by Cynthia Novack (Madison: University of Wisconsin Press, 1990). For information about contact improvisation jam classes and workshops, see www.contactimprov.net.

7. Kimberly Burke, *Lacuna* (master's thesis play, University of Texas at Austin, 2005).

8. Matthew Dickman, *Repair* (master's thesis play in progress, University of Texas at Austin, 2004).

9. Megan Gogerty, *Love Jerry* (master's thesis play, University of Texas at Austin, 2003).

CHAPTER

Dimensional Space

To see a World in a Grain of Sand
And Heaven in a Wild Flower
Hold Infinity in the palm of your hand
And Eternity in an Hour.
—William Blake

IN THE FAMOUS OPENING OF HIS POEM "THE AUGURIES OF INNOCENCE," William Blake perfectly articulates the paradox of dimensional space. In these four short lines, the delicate interplay of immensity and smallness invites us to hold the largest of concepts in the tiniest of spaces, to see profundity in simplicity, and to experience magnitude in miniature. The poem is fascinating, not only for its content but also in the story of its composition.

According to his biographer, Peter Ackroyd, Blake wrote the poem in the midst of a period of intense depression, when he was beset by financial woes, problems with his patrons, critical derision of his work, and public ridicule for his accounts of his prophetic, visionary experiences. The poem began in despair as an account of his spiritual sufferings and was titled "The Torments of Love and Jealousy." As he worked, both the tone and content of the piece began to shift in emphasis and gather velocity. He revised frantically, erasing sections, writing on top of others, drawing extraordinary sketches of surreal images in the margins. In the frantic pace of this outpouring of words and drawings, Blake seems to have crossed a deeply personal, spiritual, and psychological threshold from one dimension into another. Images of light and salvation came into the work. "The poem follows the path of his enlightenment."[1]

All writers can take comfort in Blake's experience. Even in the depths of his depression, reeling from critical derision and overwhelmed by the impossibility of making a decent living in the pursuit of his art, the poem and the process of its creation came to his rescue. The resulting work is, perhaps, his most famous: rich in allegory, filled with fantastical and prophetic revelations in surreal visual images etched in the margins. The poem speaks in multiple languages, verbal and visual, transcending any one vocabulary into multiple dimensions of expression and thought.

In this chapter we will explore dimensional space. We will look to concepts of miniature and magnitude as they are made manifest in plays that explore physical dimensions of time and space, metaphysical dimensions of fantasy and reality, and multiple stylistic genres. We will also look at the thresholds that must be crossed as one dimension leads to another. As playwrights, we are faced with the paradox that we must work on such a small scale to create the illusion of lives much larger than they really are. The interplay of large concepts in such a relatively small time and space gives live performance the powerful illusion of being so much larger than life.

MINIATURE

In *The Poetics of Space*, Gaston Bachelard takes delight in miniature space as the province of the imagination most often explored in fairy tales and fantasy. "Freed from the obligations of logical dimensions, there is a liberation that is a special characteristic of the imagination." [2] If the power of fantasy is to be fully realized, the element of amusement and the tendency to trivialize these stories must be eliminated.

There are two key concepts to attend to in the creation of miniature worlds such as those found in fairy tales and folktales: the power of manipulation of scale and the reality of fantasy. The change of scale inherent in the depiction of a miniature world provides a new way of looking at a larger society. Bachelard states, "The minuscule [is] a narrow gate that opens up an entire world." [3] Literature for both children and adults abounds with stories where the inversion of scale from large to small allows a reader or an audience to see a familiar world in a different way. In miniature, there is the possibility of parable, which provides a deeper, and perhaps more efficient, way of getting at a truth than a more realistic treatment might permit.

In theatre, this inversion of scale is often found in plays based on works of children's literature. The shrinking and growing of Alice in countless adaptations of *Alice in Wonderland*, the cozy underground domains of Ratty, Moley, and Badger in *The Wind in the Willows*, the mouse hole of *Stuart Little*, and the under-the-floorboards household of *The Borrowers* can all be created with the stage technician's magic. But what is really magical about this dimension is that the microcosm can more accurately reflect the complexities of the real world than the macrocosm. In the selection of detail we see the whole. Once we have left linear logic behind, we can begin to truly understand a different kind of truth.

Equally important to the inversion of scale is the reality of fantasy. For both children and adults, fantastical forms provide powerful metaphors that relate directly to today's society. Stories and plays that inhabit this dimension are not escapes from reality but journeys to the core of the same emotional, ethical, and political issues that concern us daily. In her acceptance speech for the National Book Award, celebrated science fiction and fantasy writer Ursula K. Le Guin stated:

> At this point realism is perhaps the least adequate means of understanding or portraying the incredible realities of our existence. . . . The fabulist, whether he uses the ancient archetype of myth and legend, or the younger ones of science and technology, may be talking as seriously as any sociologist—and a good deal more directly—about human life as it is lived, and as it might be lived, and as it ought to be lived.[4]

The journey into the dimension of fantasy is both an outward and an inward quest. Le Guin believes that "fantasy is the language of the innermost self. . . . The artist who works from the center of his [or her] own being will find archetypical images and release them into consciousness."[5]

Primary source materials from myths, legends, fairy tales, and folktales have served as the creative impetus for myriad art forms for both children and adults. Writers, composers, directors, and choreographers have used these ancient stories as touchstones for plays, operas, ballets, symphonies, films, and performance and visual art. The power of this material in a contemporary context resides in the vision, seriousness of purpose, and point of view of the artist who takes a very old story and tells it in a new way. Some writers plumb the depth of their source material and embrace the moral and ethical paradoxes it presents, while others exploit the simple story lines and broad characterizations on the superficial level of a Saturday morning cartoon. In their original form, folktales and fairy tales are often dark, violent, and morally complex, but often when they reach the stage they have been cleaned up and dumbed down, supposedly for a child audience. Usually it is adults rather than children who are uncomfortable with the raw power of the tales. The playwright dealing with this material must somehow find the central core of the story that will speak as powerfully to an audience today as it has for hundreds of years. The key, once again, is to find magnitude in miniature.

Recently, a student of mine struggled to find her own point of view in an adaptation of Hans Christian Andersen's *The Little Mermaid*.[6] The original story is a tragic tale, filled with moral ambiguity reflecting Andersen's own conflicted sense of social inferiority. The Disney animated version, while wildly popular, particularly among preadolescent girls, sanitizes the story and gives it a totally unearned happy ending. Any writer dealing with this wonderful/terrible story must deal with Andersen's original and Disney's adulterated version. In essence, *The Little Mermaid* is the story of a girl who sacrifices everything for a faithless prince and kills herself rather than kill him. What does this story have to say to young girls today? The messages are complex and conflicting. I have no doubt that my student will find her own answer, but only after she has explored the immensity of love, loss and longing, sacrifice, and self-worth. All of these issues lurk beneath the story's surface. A magnitude of ethical complexity lies within the miniature world of this simple story.

Theatre for young audiences is not the sole domain of fantasy and fable in theatre. Many serious and significant works for adult audiences draw from this wellspring of innovation and imagination. A host of experimental plays by contemporary playwrights has tapped into a fairy tale ethos with great depth and beauty. Erik Ehn's *Wolf at the Door* builds a truly terrifying tale from an initial image drawn from the story of the three little pigs. Ehn's *Red Plays* features an image of a woman sleeping in a glass casket beneath the earth, drawn straight from *Snow White*. In this same play there is a scene where a woman races pell-mell through a tunnel under the world, throwing the bones of her past abusive relationships behind her, which is reminiscent of the singing bones in *The Juniper Tree*. Caryl Churchill's *The Skriker* features a shape-shifting witch-woman, as dark and dangerous as any phantom from the Brothers Grimm. The fantasy worlds of fairy tales and folktales, myths, legends, and science fiction have rich resources for playwrights, whether the ultimate destination of the work is for children or adults. But this journey is not for the faint of heart. Do not cross the threshold unless you are prepared to deal fully with whatever you may find.

MAGNITUDE

If miniature space is at one end of the continuum of physical dimension, then magnitude, or immensity, is at the other. We experience immensity whenever an environment, an image, or an idea brings about an expansion of thought or feeling. For some, this experience is most tangible in nature, standing at the rim of the Grand Canyon, on a beach at sunset, or in the endless open desolation of the Mojave Desert. Although it may be triggered by an external stimulus, the physical sensation of immensity is an inward state of solitude and a simultaneous feeling of smallness and expansion of being.

Blake's poem urges us to see "Heaven in a Wild Flower." The notion that something so grand can be glimpsed in something so small creates the tensional force of metaphor and brings about an expansion of thought, feeling, and being. In his classic definition of tragedy, Aristotle refers to this quality as magnitude. According to Aristotle, tragedy is an imitation of an action that is complete, and whole, and of a certain magnitude . . . that can easily be embraced in one view.[7] These notions of size and scale have less to do with literal measurements in micrometers or miles and much more to do with the felt sense of expansion of thought and emotion. But even in Aristotle's time, the theatre was the place where stories of gods and humans were played out on a superhuman scale. Look to the size of their amphitheatres, carved into the sides of mountains, where thousands of spectators gathered at dawn. There is nothing small about Greek theatre. Indeed, most classical plays feature larger-than-life characters, expansive themes, and elevated language. One cannot help but wonder if these texts seemed elevated in their own time, or if it is merely our contemporary perspective that makes them seem so enormous.

What does this mean to us today? How do we conceive of the size and scale of our world? How can we fit our perceptions into our plots and plays? What is troublesome to me about a lot of writing today is exactly what is troublesome to me about our society in general: our conception of ourselves is so small. The omnipresence of television has reduced our vision to the size of a screen, even as it extends our ability to see to the ends of the earth. Modern technology has simultaneously shrunk the world to a global neighborhood and expanded our capacity to know and to experience things on the other side of the planet. The computer chip has revolutionized our conception of size as it holds ever larger amounts of information in ever smaller spaces. Cell phones, email, and the Internet put us instantly in touch with anyone anywhere on earth. Like Alice, we are caught in a Wonderland where our conceptions of time and space are simultaneously growing and shrinking. In an era when science and technology have given us so much power, why do we feel so powerless? In a contemporary landscape, what is magnitude? How do we, as writers, explore the really big ideas when the size of our thought seems so small? The answers to these questions can be found only in one word, one thought, one image at a time. Each of us can see the world in a grain of sand, if we just know how to look.

MULTIPLE DIMENSIONS

In the nineteenth century the proverbial rules of the well-made play called for unities of time, place, and action. In the narrowest sense, this meant that plays should take place in a consecutive time period, a single location, and with continuous action. In truth, relatively few plays ever followed this rigid formula. Most contemporary theatre explodes conventional notions of unity, bringing together wildly diverse times, places, historical periods, psychological states, languages, and frames of reality. The inclusion of multiple dimensions creates an exciting synergy within a play that captures the complexity and fragmentary quality of contemporary life and transcends the limitations of any single perspective or point of view.

As I look back over my own body of work as a playwright, I realize that every play I have ever written contains a central conflict involving two or more dimensions: fantasy and reality, fiction and history, past and present, living and dead, and deaf and hearing worlds combine and collide in play after play. Perhaps because I have written so much of this work for young audiences, I have felt somehow liberated from the confines of ordinary time and place and have found a continual source of inspiration in the time between times and the spaces between places. These plays have offerd me an invitation to cross the borders of my imagination frequently and at will.

Theatre for adults is also filled with wonderful examples of the effective use of multiple dimensions. Caryl Churchill's *Cloud Nine* brings colonial and contemporary characters together as they slide through centuries and switch genders at intermission. Arthur Kopit's *Wings* takes us into the mind of a stroke victim and juxtaposes the netherworld of her aphasia in sharp contrast with the ordered medical world of her caregivers. Tony Kushner's epic *Angels in America* brings historical and fictional figures, gay and straight characters, ethereal and earthbound worlds together with power and passion. The strength of this huge play lies not in any single strand of its story, but in the complex weaving of multiple times and places and dimensions of reality.

Psychological states may be considered dimensions made manifest in levels of consciousness. Every human being and, potentially, every character, exists on conscious, unconscious, and subconscious levels. Many playwrights depict only the conscious dimensions of their characters, but the characters' motivations are often fueled by subconscious needs and desires. Some plays depict a character's alter ego as a separate character or use a dream sequence to bring the unconscious realm to light.

Some writers have taken the notion of multiple dimensions even further to include works that are partially devised or compiled from diverse sources not of the playwright's creation. In his book *New Playwriting Strategies*, Paul Castagno refers to these plays as hybrids. "The hybrid play is a literary and theatrical crossbreed, a blending of genres and disparate sources both textural and performative. In many cases, the sources are unrelated and may appear given to arbitrary selection."[8] Charles Mee's *Trojan Women* combines fragments of the ancient Greek play by Euripides with sections of testimony from Bosnian refugees and popular songs.

In other hybrid plays writers use source materials as central elements but create a new context around them, inviting us to look at these sources in an entirely different way. In a recent playwriting workshop I taught, Carson Kreitzer, a Playwriting Fellow at the Michener Center for Writers, chose to write about the imponderable phenomenon of women who kill their children. In her provocative play 1:23, she draws from multiple sources including verbatim sections of the actual testimony of Andrea Yates, the Houston woman who was convicted of drowning her five young children in the bathtub. Using this harrowing account as a baseline, Kreitzer adds a simultaneous story based on Susan Smith's murder of her children and her subsequent attempt to blame it on an African American carjacker. She finally weaves in a third thread of Juana, a Texas woman who tried to drown herself and her seven children, as a contemporary manifestation of La Llorona, the legendary weeping woman who mourns the children she murdered. At various points, Kreitzer touches in a leitmotif of biblical verses all drawn from chapter 1: verse 23 from both Old and New Testament scriptures. These numbers 1:23 echo the time of Yates' transcript: 1:23 P.M. Astonishingly, the biblical verses fit the horrendous circumstances with which they are juxtaposed with chilling accuracy.[9] This fascinating play brings together fact and fiction, testimony and poetry, real and imagined characters with heartbreaking humanity and a surprising sense of cohesion.

Take a moment to think of your own work. What are the dimensions that you consistently explore in the worlds you create? How do they intersect or collide, and what are the ways your characters and your audiences move from one dimension to another?

THRESHOLDS

When we pass from one dimension into another, we invariably cross a threshold of some kind. In physical space, it may be a door, or a window, or the flap of a tent that separates outside from inside. In psychological terms, a threshold is that portal of perception that permits access from the conscious mind into the unconscious or subconscious by way of dream, or drug, or the post-hypnotic suggestion of a therapist. In metaphysical terms, a threshold may be a state of grace, or prayer, or meditation that transports the believer from one spiritual space to another.

In the theatre there are also physical, psychological, and spiritual thresholds within the playwright, the play, and, finally, the performance. All of them are related and connected, like a series of portals that permit access into the world of the play. For the playwright in the act of creation, the first threshold is deeply personal. The writer must be willing to step out of the comfort zone of what he or she has written before into the space of the unknown, into the liminal space between an idea and its execution. Philosopher Thomas Moore, in his article "Neither Here nor There," describes this passage eloquently:

> There are places in this world that are neither here nor there, neither up nor down, neither real nor imaginary. These are the in-between places, difficult to find and even more challenging to sustain. Yet they are the most fruitful places of all. For in these liminal narrows a kind of life takes place that is out of the ordinary, creative, and once in a while genuinely magical.[10]

In some plays, passage from one dimension to another happens by way of a transition: a spell, a charm, moving through a wardrobe, falling down a rabbit hole. In many contemporary plays, there are no transitions, no dividing lines between dimensions that mix and blend and bump up against each other. The synergy between conflicting times, places, languages, sources, and multiple points of view creates a forward momentum of thought and theme.

The final threshold is, of course, in performance. Every architectural element in a traditional theatre environment is designed to provide a different kind of threshold, to focus attention on the playing space, and to move the audience from the real world of the auditorium into the fictional world of the play. As the house lights dim and preshow music begins, spectators enter the world of the play on a beam of light and a wave of sound. Even in nontraditional spaces where there is little or no separation between the audience and the performers, there is the threshold of a willing suspension of disbelief that must be crossed at the start of the performance.

Some plays offer easy access through an empathetic character or a compelling plot, but some plays are more complex than others and require more effort and attention from the spectator. The notion of access is as tricky for the playwright as it is for the audience, especially in nontraditional, nonlinear, polyvocal, or hybrid pieces. When I am working with a writer on such material, I often ask questions like, "How much access do you want your audience to have?" and "Do you want people to understand what is going on in the play or merely to experience it?" Some plays and performances invite access through ideas while others create emotional bonds; still others use political activism and social issues to establish connections, but thresholds are a matter of mutual responsibility shared by both the playwright and the audience. In even the most opaque experimental plays, the writer is rarely deliberately trying to prevent access or to keep the spectator outside the world of the play. Playwrights often tell me that they want each audience member to find his or her own meaning. This is fine, but if *any* meaning is to be found, it is also the responsibility of the playwright to clarify his or her *own* meaning or intention first. A threshold must be created if it is to be crossed.

In this chapter we have examined physical dimensions of miniature and magnitude, temporal dimensions of past, present, and future, psychological dimensions of consciousness, and metaphysical dimensions of fantasy and reality, fact and fiction. We have also considered theatrical dimensions of multiple styles and genres, which might be combined in a single work to great effect. In the following sections we shall try to make these concepts concrete in exercises based on Awareness Through Movement, a body-mind discipline developed by Moshe Feldenkrais, and in activities that allow you to experience miniature space and concepts of magnitude and immensity in your own writing. When dealing with matters of size and scale, it is one thing to visualize very large and very small spaces but another thing to experience them. Some of the following activities will involve building tiny spaces and imagining the characters who might live there and events that might transpire within. Other activities will encourage you to go to a location that inspires feelings of intimate immensity to see what ideas might be waiting there for you to find.

MOVEMENT: FELDENKRAIS AWARENESS THROUGH MOVEMENT AND FUNCTIONAL INTEGRATION

In this section we will explore another mind-body discipline that Jim has used to help actors and writers build personal awareness and improve physical functioning.[11] Thinking and consciously responding to thought are key concepts in the work of Moshe Feldenkrais. Using thought in conjunction with movement can help an individual release tension, balance the body's energies, and organize the nervous system. In these exercises, movement is experienced first in the body and then re-created in the mind in every kinesthetic detail. Thought innervates muscle and, in Feldenkrais work, the constant interplay of thinking and movement can bring about changes that are both physical and mental, promoting spontaneity and wholeness.

Jim likes to say, "Habit is stronger than God," indicating that habitual self-use will feel comfortable and right even if it is physiologically harmful. Change, even if it is better for the body, will often feel awkward and incorrect at first because it is unfamiliar. When the body is free, it is expansive; there is a sense of magnitude in both muscles and mind. When the body is held or stressed, it becomes compressed and an interior space is diminished. Exploration of Feldenkrais techniques can help writers step out of their habitual comfort zone, where nonthinking resides, and consciously experience physical states where discoveries of new physical patterns of awareness can be found.

Shoulders, Neck, and Scapulae

Lie on your back with your knees toward the ceiling and your feet flat on the floor.

Place both arms above the chest, reaching toward the ceiling, while releasing both shoulders into the floor.

Begin small circles (rotations) with the arms; release your shoulders into the floor.

Reverse the direction.

While lying on the floor, roll to the right side.

Allow the head to rest on the floor while the right arm is extended in front of the torso, palm up.

Extend the left arm above the body, toward the ceiling, arm turned so the palm is facing the front of the body.

Lift the left arm out of the shoulder and take it toward the right arm, allowing it to touch the right arm or hand.

Return to the original extended-arm-above-the-body position.

Repeat several times. You will find that the arm will be able to reach farther and farther with each repetition.

Leave the arm touching the right hand and/or the floor, and while keeping the left palm flat on the floor, begin sliding it along the floor until it reaches the head; then turn the palm up (which rotates the shoulder) and continue the circle with the extended left arm.

The head rotates with the arm and the eyes continue to follow the arm as far as possible.

This will require some rotation of the torso, but keep the hips in place, lying on the right side.

Once the arm reaches the back side of the body, rotate the arm so the palm moves across the thigh onto the floor in front of the body, now joining the right arm. This completes a full circle, with two rotations of the arm in the shoulder. Repeat several times.

Now turn onto your left side and raise your right hand in the air.

Without actually moving, **think** through the entire process on this side, being careful not to leave out any details.

Repeat this several times.

Now, physically execute the entire sequence on the left side and see if there is greater ease than when you first experienced this movement.

Lower Back and Lumbar

Writers tend to tense the lower back (lumbar region). This is the result of tilting the pelvis down and deepening the lumbar; or tilting the lumbar up, resulting in a compression of the entire torso. The following exercises are designed to release the pelvis into an aligned position and reduce the tension.

Lie on your back with your knees toward the ceiling and your feet flat on the floor.

Imagine a clock face reflected on the ceiling.

Tilt your pelvis enough to clear the floor and tilt it precisely toward each number on the clock. For example, twelve o'clock is up toward the head; six o'clock is down toward the floor; nine o'clock is directly to the midside and three o'clock is directly opposite.

There will be subtle tilts and movements; explore each number/position on the clock face and then make combinations to suit your imagination. Visualize the clock face and think through each movement as you shift from one position to another.

Maintain the same position as stated above.

Place the legs together and drop the knees to one side. Remember to tilt the pelvis toward the head before dropping the knees to the side.

Allow the opposite arm to lengthen down toward the heels.

Keep the arm fully on the mat as it reaches downward toward the foot.

Keep the head in the center for several repetitions.

Then take the head to the same side as the knees for several repetitions.

Now, move the head in opposition to the legs.

Once the legs are dropped to the side, return the head to its center position; cease the stretching of the arm, then return the knees.

Before you repeat this exercise on the opposite side of the body, take a moment to scan the body in your mind and visualize each step of the process.

Repeat with the other direction and side of the body.

Move onto your hands and knees.

Make a V with your arms, one hand on top of the other and a V with your legs. Place the forehead on the hands and roll the head forward until you are near the crown of the head, then roll the head back until you cross the forehead and your face is near the mat.

Your weight is supported by the forearms and the legs (knees).

Lengthen through the back and keep the lower ribs from dropping toward the floor, especially when dropping back toward the feet.

Take a moment to scan the body and think through the movement.

Repeat several times.

Shoulders, Torso, Pelvis

This activity is useful for the upper body from the head and neck, down the torso, and into the pelvic girdle. There is also some involvement of the eyes.

Sit on the floor.

Bend the left leg in front of the body so that the foot is inside the right thigh of the leg, which is bent beneath you.

You will be sitting on the left hip although you should try to distribute your weight as equally as possible.

Place the right arm in front of the body with the elbow bent so the inside of the arm and palm are facing the torso. (Your arm is in a sphere.)

Reach down with your left arm and place your hand on the floor to give you support and to keep your body upright.

Leading with the right hip, lift it and move it to the left, allowing your right arm, head, and torso to continue this movement.

Keep the left arm on the floor, supporting you as you turn around.

Don't lean to the left if you can help it.

Allow the right hip to initiate the movement to return to center, to your original position.

Keep repeating this same movement, noticing how much farther you can turn with every repetition.

Allow your eyes to follow the right hand.

Change legs so you are sitting on your right hip with the right leg bent in front. Raise your left arm in the sphere in front with the inside facing the torso.

Before you initiate any physical movement, take a moment to scan the body and re-create the entire procedure in every kinesthetic detail in your thinking.

Do not hurry or skip any details of the original movement.

Repeat the twisting and reaching sequence several times in your mind.

Don't forget your eyes as they now follow the left hand.

Physically repeat the entire movement sequence once or twice.

You should find that you will be able to move farther to the right on the first actual movement than you were able to do when you moved to the left for the first time a moment ago.

The visualization and thinking through the movement, prior to actual execution, should have made this motion easier and more efficient.

DIMENSIONAL SPACE EXERCISES

Miniature Worlds

Model building for theatrical sets is a crucial part of the design process. Once the physical dimensions of a scenic design can be seen in miniature form, it is possible to see how the set might actually function. The models you will build for this exercise are *not* set designs; they are tiny worlds. These activities may be done before a play is written or at any time during the process of creation. Some of my students have created the world first and then written a play inspired by the model. The point here is to express how this tiny world feels, to discover its colors, textures, shapes, and perhaps, even sounds. I encourage you to think big as you think small and not to be dissuaded from what might seem to be impossible. In the world of your imagination, the only impossibility is a failure to dream.

There are two possible beginnings to this activity. The first starts with a vision, the second with a space. To start with a vision:

In the eye of your mind, visualize the world that you will create in miniature. See it in as much detail as possible.

If it is helpful to do so, sketch your feelings and impressions of this world as an analog drawing.

Do *not* use words to describe this world. Keep this experience visual and kinesthetic.

In a space no larger than a shoe box (smaller if possible), build a representation of this world. Try to use only three-dimensional objects and building materials rather than photographic images (e.g., clay, balsa wood, buttons, pins, marbles, pieces of glass, mirrors, lighting gels, jelly beans, twigs, leaves, acorns, seeds, nuts, etc.).

If you start with the world:

> Find a tiny object that you think might contain or hold a world within it: (an egg, shell, bone, seedpod, tiny bowl, ice cube tray, tube, and so on).
>
> Visualize the world that might inhabit this space.
>
> Follow all of the steps above to build the world inside the object.
>
> As you build these worlds, remember to leave room for inhabitants.

Writing from the Worlds

> Place your miniature world in front of you.
>
> Take three to five minutes to write down what you see when you look into your world.
>
> Limit yourself to *only* what your senses could perceive here.
>
> Imagine that you see a being in your world. It may be human, animal, or totally imaginary. Write answers to the following questions and prompts:
>
>> What does it look like? Where is it? What is it doing?
>>
>> How does it feel about being there?
>>
>> Give the being a name. Give the being a wish.
>>
>> Give the being a need. Give the being a fear.
>>
>> Give the being a gift, talent, or ability.
>
> Imagine another being in your world.
>
>> What does it look like? Where is it? What is it doing?
>>
>> How does it feel about being there?
>>
>> Give the being a name. Give the being a wish.
>>
>> Give the being a need. Give the being a fear.
>>
>> Give the being a gift, talent, or ability.
>
> Imagine a conflict between these two beings or a conflict between them and the world.
>
> Write a play that deals with these two beings in this world; use only one page.
>
> Write another play that deals with these two beings in this world; use only half a page.
>
> Write another play that deals with these two beings in this world; use only three lines of dialogue and no more than three actions.

Experiencing Immensity

As was the case with miniature space, the experience of immensity is best accomplished in an actual physical environment. For these activities you must
go to a space where you feel that sense of expansion of thought and being
that Bachelard refers to as "intimate immensity." The sheer size of the space
is less important than the way it makes you feel. It may be an outside space,
like a forest, open field, or hilltop. You may decide to go to this space at night
when the sky is filled with stars. If so, be sure to bring a flashlight so you can
write. Your space may also be indoors: a temple, cathedral, theatre, rotunda,
banquet hall, power plant. What is important is that the space must fill you
with some kind of awe. It may be that the space makes you uncomfortable or
upset in some way. Your perception should be one of magnitude.

Find a place in the space where you can sit for a period of time. Take a few
moments to jot down your primary sensory responses to this space.

How is your body different here than in other places?

How is your thought different here than in other places?

Imagine lines radiating outward from your body to the farthest extremities
of the space.

Does the space make you feel powerful, or do you feel insignificant in
the presence of immensity?

Imagine a being in this space.

What does it look like? Where is it? What is it doing?

How does it feel about being there?

Give the being a name. Give the being a wish.

Give the being a need. Give the being a fear.

Give the being a gift, talent, or ability.

Imagine another being in this space.

What does it look like? Where is it? What is it doing?

How does it feel about being there?

Give the being a name. Give the being a wish.

Give the being a need. Give the being a fear.

Give the being a gift, talent, or ability.

Imagine a conflict between these two beings.

Write a play that deals with these two beings in this world; use only three lines of dialogue and no more than three actions.

Write another play that deals with these two beings in this world; use a full page.

Write a third play that deals with these two beings in this world; use as many pages as you need.

Thresholds and Multiple Dimensions

In your life:

For five minutes, write in stream of consciousness what the word *threshold* means at this moment in your life.

Make a list of the thresholds you have crossed in the past year.

Make a list of the thresholds you still have to cross in the next year.

Make a list of the thresholds you visualize yourself crossing in the next twenty years.

In your work:

Make a list of all the dimensions that appear and recur in your plays.

Make a list of all the thresholds that appear and recur in your plays.

Make a list of the dimensions and thresholds that you would like to explore in future plays.

Crossing Thresholds

From a play on which you are currently working, create a scene in which two or more dimensions are made manifest and a threshold is crossed from one dimension to another. Possible dimensions include:

Size: miniature, magnitude

Time: past, present, future

Psychology: conscious, unconscious, subconscious

Metaphysical: fantasy, reality; fictional, actual

Remember, crossing thresholds into multiple dimensions is a bit different from crossing physical territories or personal boundaries, as we did in the previous chapter. Territories and boundaries tend to be related to characters, whereas dimensions deal with the larger worlds, genres, and styles of the play as a whole.

Write a scene that would *never* take place in the play.

Write a scene that might actually take place in the play.

A WORD OR TWO . . .

As a teacher of playwriting and a dramaturg, my biggest challenge is not helping playwrights develop analytic acumen, critical faculties, or a sense of structure and technique. The hardest part of working with young, and not so young, writers is helping them look within themselves and believe in the possibility of magnitude in their lives and in their work. To do this, they must be able to look beyond the surface of what they have seen on television, in film, and often in theatre; explore material that has mythic dimension, personal relevance, and ethical complexity; and abandon the safety of distance and irony in the pursuit of an expansion of thought that can truly be called immense.

NOTES

1. Peter Ackroyd, *Blake* (New York: Knopf, 1996), 278.

2. Gaston Bachelard, *The Poetics of Space: The Classic Look at How We Experience Intimate Places*, trans. Maria Jolas (Boston: Beacon, 1995), 149.

3. Ibid., 155.

4. Ursula K. Le Guin, *The Language of the Night: Essays on Fantasy and Science Fiction* (New York: Perigee, 1980), 58.

5. Ibid., 78.

6. Jennifer Cameron, *The Little Mermaid* (master's thesis play, University of Texas at Austin, 2005).

7. Aristotle, *Poetics* (New York: Hill and Wang, 1969), 66.

8. Paul Castagno, *New Playwriting Strategies: A Language-Based Approach to Playwriting* (New York: Routledge, 2001), 35–36.

9. Carson Kreitzer, 1:23 (play in progress, University of Texas at Austin, 2004).

10. Thomas Moore, "Neither Here nor There: Psychotherapy and Religion Provide Tools for Deepening the Soul," *Parabola: Myth, Tradition, and the Search for Meaning* 25, no. 1 (2000): 34.

11. For more information about the Feldenkrais system, see *Awareness Through Movement*, by Moshe Feldenkrais (San Francisco: HarpersSanFrancisco, 1991).

$$6$$

CHAPTER

Sacred and Mythic Space

IN THE EMPTY SPACE, DIRECTOR PETER BROOK STATES THAT THE
stage is a place where the invisible can be made visible in a "Holy Theatre"
that speaks to deep yearnings human beings have felt for a spiritual connection to forces larger than themselves.[1] The links between theatre and
rituals of worship, ceremony, and celebration reach back to the very beginnings of recorded time, long before the ancient Greeks formalized performance in festivals growing out of Dionysian rites and rituals. In their most
elemental form, the rituals of sympathetic magic performed by a tribal shaman to ensure the success of a hunt provided all the basic elements of theatre. These ceremonies involved role taking in which celebrants enacted the
actions of stalking and killing prey that they hoped to replicate in the actual
hunt. The key element in these enactments was the belief that the ceremony actually accomplished something that would have tangible results
when the hunting party went out into the forest. The enactment served as a
way for the tribal members to exert some control over elements that seem
to be beyond control.

Throughout history, theatre has always shared similar elements with sacred practices, including scripted or rehearsed texts, costumes, music,
dance, and, most important, the presence of live celebrants and an audience
of onlookers willing to accept the premise that the actions they are witness-
ing have a significance beyond the surface of their pretense. Even the most
secular forms of theatre demand a leap of some kind of faith from audience
members, who, for the moment, are willing to believe in the fictionalized truth
before them.

CONSTRUCTED SACRED SPACE

Practices of worship and ritual usually take place in spaces created specifically for that purpose. The ritual circle of beaten earth in the middle of a tribal village, the innermost chamber of the great pyramids of Egypt, the altar of a tiny country church in New Hampshire, and the basilica of the Vatican in Rome all have in common that they were constructed as sacred spaces given meaning by the activities and associations of believers. These spaces are special, set apart from the daily activities of ordinary time. They have no tangible purpose other than to provide a gathering place for those who share similar beliefs and customs. They are the thresholds that provide access to unseen realms of spiritual significance and differentiate between sacred and profane space.

According to Romanian philosopher Mircea Eliade, sacred space provides a culture with a fixed point in the universe and a center of belief. Profane space, on the other hand, is a chaos of "undifferentiated nothingness." One of the primary functions of sacred space is to give a sense of order to the universe and some notion of how one fits into a pattern larger than oneself.[2] Geographer Yi-Fu Tuan echoes this notion in his suggestion that mythic space helps provide a worldview or cosmology that serves as a culture's more or less systematic attempt to make sense of its environment.[3]

Although sacred spaces have many manifestations, there are astonishing similarities between the structures created by diverse cultures to express and contain their worship. Whether it is a natural space imbued with sacred significance by a native people, an ancient Chinese temple, or a vast cathedral built to glorify the power and authority of a Christian religion, most sacred spaces have a focal point that directs attention to the primary celebrant. This central axis is quite literally a representation of the *axis mundi*, or world center, "the cosmic pillar, or the world tree, which connects earth with heaven."[4] Most sacred spaces also have special areas marking the four directions of north, south, east, and west. The Native American medicine wheel identifies each of these cardinal points with an animal totem and with particular colors, natural forces, seasons, and desired human attributes such as vision, passion, intuition, and wisdom. Most medieval cathedrals feature a central altar surrounded by architectural features of the nave and apse and side chapels, which mark the cardinal directions and replicate the shape of a crucifix. Most sacred spaces contain some kind of object at the focal point: an icon, book, scroll, or tablet.

In the same way that sacred space exists to focus the attention of celebrants upon a holy object or a ritual activity, theatrical space is constructed to focus the attention of an audience upon a performance. In most theatres there are separate areas for spectators and celebrants and all atmospheric elements such as masking, lighting, and sound serve to diminish the presence and prominence of the spectator and to place greater emphasis on the performers.

In the classical French theatre of the Comedie Francaise, an actor pounds a staff on the floor of the stage three times before each performance, a gesture that harkens back to evoking the presence of a god. In both sacred and theatrical space, the enactment is something apart from the everyday, a sacred act that invites the presence of a higher power.

ARCHETYPES

Most cultures communicate the tenets of their belief systems and ethical values by telling stories. Be they in the form of biblical parables, passages from the Koran or Torah, or the teachings of Buddha, sacred stories usually instruct by example.

The characters who inhabit sacred texts often take the form of archetypes. The concept of the archetype is found in psychology, literature, history, religion, and art. It refers to an elemental force or image that is replicated in many different forms. According to Jung, an archetype is the articulation of an energy that springs from the same need that motivates humans to build sacred spaces: a desire to understand the universe. Archetypes originate in the collective unconscious of humankind. They belong to no single culture but are found in the religions, myths, legends, fairy tales, and dreams of all cultures.[5] Archetypes such as the trickster, magician, crone, and maiden find incarnation in a vast catalog of characters. The Native American trickster is Raven. In Norse folktales, he is Loki. In the fairy tales of central Europe, he is Reynard the Fox, and in the American South, he goes by the name of Br'er Rabbit. Archetypes can embody both the positive and negative aspects of the same character in different forms. The archetype of the crone is the witch Baba Yaga, but her positive energy is also embodied in Mother Earth. The magician is both Merlin and Faust. The archetype is an image belonging to the whole human race, but the embodiment of that image is specific and localized in the stories, plays, and sacred texts of specific cultures.

Much of the canon of dramatic literature is built upon characters that are consciously or unconsciously crafted from archetypes. Most ancient Greek plays are based upon mythic sources or upon historical events told in the language of myth. Medieval mystery and miracle plays are drawn directly from events from the Old and New Testaments. The epic *Mahabharata* from India, and Japanese Noh plays are filled with gods and heroes and a host of archetypical characters. But archetypes do not belong only to ancient sources; they are also the stuff of popular culture and contemporary theatre. In her play *Polaroid Stories*, Naomi Iizuka tells the tales of real teenagers living on the streets, but the characters in her contempory underworld are drawn from classical mythology. In a 1999 article in *American Theatre*, Iizuka states, "Myth reminds us of the unknown in the quotidian, the seed of the unfamiliar buried in the everyday. Myths ask simple questions, as simple as they are necessary, as necessary as they are hard. Our hearts crack open in the asking."[6]

As playwrights, it is important that we understand and familiarize ourselves with the concept of archetypes and know how to differentiate them from stereotypes. An archetype embodies the original source of the power of a cultural image. Although its form is specific and localized, its energy is timeless. Archetypal characters are fully developed with dimensionality, power, magnitude, and a sense of completeness. A stereotype, on the other hand, is a character that is insufficiently developed for the context in which it appears. It is often a shallow or predictable caricature, defined by one or two surface characteristics that come to stand for the full dimension of the character. The trickster is an archetype who goes by many names in many different stories. Television sitcoms are filled with dumb blondes and nincompoop neighbors who are deliberately, or accidentally, crafted as stereotypes.

Think for a moment about your own plays. What archetypes do you find there? Which stereotypes might you develop further? What do your characters worship? What ceremonies of enactment do they perform? Whether the play is as overtly mythic as Mary Zimmerman's *Metamorphosis*, or as deliberately domestic as Edward Albee's *Who's Afraid of Virginia Woolf?*, sacred ceremonies of death and rebirth are enacted even in the most modern dress. It is up to us to clarify the catechism of our craft.

THE STRUCTURE OF SACRED STORIES

Just as there are spatial similarities in the construction of sacred spaces and cultural connections between archetypes, there are also patterns of common elements and events in the myths, sacred stories, folktales and fairy tales from many different traditions. In *The Hero with a Thousand Faces*, Joseph

Campbell presents an exhaustive study of Eastern and Western mythologies and traces recurring elements that appear in widely different cultures and are embodied in the nuclear unit of the monomyth:

> A hero ventures forth from the world of the common day into a region of supernatural wonder: fabulous forces are there encountered and a decisive victory is won: the hero comes back from this mysterious adventure with the power to bestow boons on his fellow man.[7]

Within this open-ended framework, the monomyth usually contains the same basic characters and events.

The Hero: A man or woman of exceptional gifts, which are often unrecognized or disdained, who is able to battle past personal limitations to go on a journey for the good of the larger society.

Supernatural Aid: A protective figure who provides the adventurer with a magic charm, amulet, aid, or information to help along the way.

Old God/Crone: The ogre or wise aspect of the father or mother—often the antagonist or redeemer.

Goddess: The good or bad mother or the virgin bride with whom a mystical marriage or reunion takes place. She may also be a temptress.

Ultimate Boon: The subject of the quest, which may be a gift or curse.

The journey of the hero usually follows the same pattern or series of stages.

Call to Adventure: Something happens to upset the universe—a crisis, chance, or blunder. Destiny summons the hero, who accepts or refuses the call. If the call is refused, the adventure is converted to its negative.

First Threshold: The passage from one world into the next.

Belly of the Whale: The hero dies or is swallowed into unknown or unconscious forces, to be rescued or reborn anew.

Road of Trials: The series of miraculous tests and ordeals, monsters to be battled, tasks to be accomplished, deeds to be done.

Apotheosis: The ultimate battle resulting in atonement (at-one-ment) with the father or the meeting with or marriage to the goddess.

Return: A reentry into the world left behind.

Homecoming: The hero is welcomed or reviled, celebrated or banished.

The structure of Campbell's monomyth has much in common with the configuration of Aristotelian plot structure. An initial state of balance is upset by an inciting event (the call). This causes the protagonist to confront the antagonistic force (First Threshold) and triggers a series of events constituting the rising action (Road of Trials). Eventually this culminates in a climax (Apotheosis), which in turn brings about a reversal (Atonement/Marriage). This brings about the events constituting the falling action (Return), leading to a resolution in which a new state of balance is achieved (Homecoming).

It is not surprising that these two structures should mirror each other so completely, since both are essentially based on the same sources. Aristotle's *Poetics* provides the ingredients for the basic elements of structure, which have endured even to this day. The *Poetics* is thought to be fragments from an unfinished manuscript or a set of lecture notes that describes the theatre that Aristotle saw around him. Since most of that theatre was based on mythic sources and sacred stories, it is no wonder that these elements should follow the same basic pattern as the monomyth.

As playwrights, we chart the course of our characters through a series of events that change them or their worlds in substantial and meaningful ways. Whether they are heroes in the traditional sense, or antiheroes, or simply people struggling to get through the day, the magnitude of their endeavors is a measure of the depth of the plays that contain them. The plotting of a dramatic action is a series of interrelated choices, and each part of the hero's journey has an impact on every other part of the story. Many plays contain elements of myth and archetype, even in most contemporary settings. The roads of trials traveled by Willy Loman in *Death of a Salesman* and by Professor Vivian Bearing in Margaret Edson's *Wit* are no less harrowing than those faced by Orpheus or Persephone. Without the playwright's intensity of vision, clarity of depiction, and ability to elevate illness into art, Willy Loman would be just another old man with Alzheimer's disease and Professor Bearing just another cancer statistic.

In the activities that follow, we will explore techniques of finding the invisible in the visible through movement with a greater awareness of our kinesthetic bodies. This work builds upon the connection between thought and movement found in the Feldenkrais techniques discussed in the previous chapter and adds the element of visualization.

I will also present the most important playwriting exercise I have found in all my years of teaching to help clarify the relationship of form and content in dramatic structure. This activity draws its inspiration from an ancient tool of divination: reading tarot cards. I have used it in virtually every class I have taught in the past decade with astonishing results. Finally, we will look at ways to connect the elements of Campbell's monomyth to your own plays by articulating the journeys of the heroes you have created in mythic terms.

MOVEMENT: KINESTHETIC IMAGINATION

The word *kinesthesia* literally means the perception or sensing of the motion, weight, or position of the body as muscles, tendons and joints move. The kinesthetic body is the perceptual body that we envision in our imagination, not simply as a visual experience but as a felt sense of motion. Visualization techniques are found in many diverse disciplines, from sports, to psychotherapy, to medicine. In competitive sports, an athlete will visualize every element of an intended pole vault or broad jump before actually executing the activity. The psychotherapist helps a client deal with fears and phobias by leading the client through a series of visualizations where each fear or phobia is confronted and overcome. Cancer patients are taught to battle the invisible forces raging within their bodies by visualizing cellular warfare and the defeat of the monsters of malignancy. This rehearsal is not unlike the sympathetic magic of the shaman. The key is belief in the possibility of a successful outcome.

Cultivation of kinesthetic imagination is important for performers and writers. Actors and dancers use these techniques to overcome stage fright. For writers, the ability to feel the momentum of scenes and to experience the emotional dynamics felt by characters brings an immediacy and intensity to the writing process. The kinesthetic imagination can be exercised just like any muscle. The strength and specificity of visualizations come from repeated practice. As it was with Developmental Movement, the key is trust. Skepticism and doubt are self-induced blockades to the full exercise of our capacity to imagine. The experience of the kinesthetic body requires a willingness to trust that the invisible can be experienced as fully as the visible in the eye of the mind.

Kinesthetic Body

This activity was created by Jean Houston and is described in *The Possible Human*. According to Houston, "The activation of the kinesthetic imagination serves to enable the part of brain functioning that stores optimal images of performance to re-educate, as it were, the part of the motor cortex that involves the usual performance."[8] These exercises take a bit of practice. For some people the experience of moving from the literal body into the kinesthetic body is very difficult, as it requires both a separation of mind and body and an integration of both. It becomes easier with repetition over time, so do not be discouraged if this is difficult at first. It may also be helpful to practice with movements that have a tangible result, like a tennis swing or an exercise routine. The more the kinesthetic body is exercised, the more flexible and responsive it will become! Have fun with this! The following is taken directly from *The Possible Human*.

Check to see if your weight is evenly balanced on both your feet and sense your feet in contact with the ground.

Scan your body to ensure that you have relaxed any unnecessary tension, particularly in your shoulders and neck area.

Raise your *real* right arm and stretch, sensing the shifting alignment of the muscles all over your body as you do this. Feel the stretch in your fingers, your hand, your arm, your shoulders, your torso. Now, with equal awareness, lower your arm.

Repeat this several times.

Now stretch your *kinesthetic* right arm, allowing yourself to experience this as vividly as possible.

Stretch again with your *real* arm, then your *kinesthetic* arm.

Alternate several times between stretching with your *real* arm and your *kinesthetic* arm.

Do the same thing with your *real* left arm and your *kinesthetic* left arm, always remembering to experience your *kinesthetic* arm with as much reality as you had when you were stretching your *real* arm.

Do the same thing, *alternately* stretching *real* and *kinesthetic* arms.

Let your *real* arms and shoulders circle in a round forward movement like the paddlewheels of a steamboat.

Do the same thing with your *kinesthetic* arms and shoulders, continuing to feel the same momentum you felt with your *real* arms and shoulders.

Alternate.

Let your *real* arms and shoulders circle in a backward motion.

Do the same thing kinesthetically.

Alternate.

Now, with your *real* body, make a fencing lunge to the right.

Come back to the center.

Repeat this several times.

Now lunge to the right with your *kinesthetic* body.

Come back to the center.

Alternate several times between your *real* and *kinesthetic* bodies.

Do the same thing with a fencing lunge to the left.

Follow this sequence:

Real body lunges to the right.

Back to the center.

Real body lunges to the left.

Back.

Kinesthetic body lunges to the left.

Back.

Real body lunges to the left.

Back.

Kinesthetic body lunges to the right and comes back.

Real body lunges to the right and comes back.

Real body lunges to the left.

Back.

Now, *at the same time*, your *kinesthetic* body lunges to the right and your *real* body lunges to the left.

Come back to center.

Now lunge with your *real* body to the right and your *kinesthetic* body to the left.

Come back to center.

Rest for a moment.

Raise both the *real* arms over your head and hold them there.

At the same time feel your *kinesthetic* arms hanging at your sides.

Slowly lower your *real* arms while you raise your *kinesthetic* arms, putting as much attention into your *kinesthetic* arms as you direct to your *real* arms.

Now, lower your *kinesthetic* arms while you raise your *real* arms.

Lower your *real* arms while you raise your *kinesthetic* arms.

Continue with this until the raising and lowering of your *kinesthetic* arms becomes almost indistinguishable from the movement of your *real* arms.

Rest.

Be aware of the space several feet in front of you. Now with your *real* body, jump as high as you can into that space.

Jump back.

Do it again with your *real* body, jumping as high as you can, forward and back.

Do the same thing with your *kinesthetic* body, forward and back.

Now do it with your *real* body.

Real body again.

Real body again.

Kinesthetic body, jumping as high as you can, forward and back.

Real body.

Kinesthetic body.

Jump forward with your *kinesthetic* body and stay there.

Now, jumping as high as you can, jump with your *real* body *into* your *kinesthetic* body!

Standing still, notice how you feel. Close your eyes.

Scan your body again.

Is there greater awareness in your body?

Begin to walk around and notice your awareness.

Opening your eyes, see if your perception of the external world and others has changed at all.[9]

SACRED AND MYTHIC SPACE EXERCISES

The Tarot

The following exercise draws inspiration from an ancient, mythic method of divination: the tarot. The reading of tarot cards can be traced back as far as the ancient Egyptians and appears in many Eastern and Western cultures. The tarot deck is made up of seventy-eight cards that bear evocative images, symbols, and pictures of archetypal figures and forces. In a typical tarot reading, a questioner comes to a reader with a problem or situation that needs clarification. The questioner shuffles and selects a number of cards without seeing their faces. The reader turns the cards over, lays them out in a particular order around a significator card, and interprets their meaning. Each position in the layout calls for a different kind of information contributing to the question or situation under examination. The relevance of a reading comes not in a single meaning or message, but in the sense the questioner makes of the many meanings suggested by the reader as possible interpretations of the relationship between the imagery of the cards and their position in the layout.

The following layout has been adapted from the Motherpeace Tarot.[10] I like this layout because it has a circular rather than a linear pattern, which clearly demonstrates how each card relates to every other card. For the purposes of this exercise, you will not be using actual tarot cards with predetermined

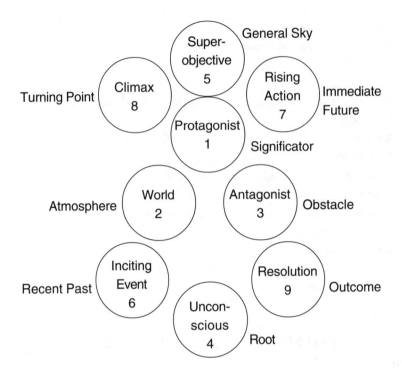

images and iconography; you will create your own cards, either in words or in pictures, depicting parts of a play you have in progress. For example, on the first card you will write or draw words or images that capture the essence of the protagonist, or central character or characters in your play. On subsequent cards you will write words or draw images suggesting other parts of your play, such as the antagonist, unconscious forces, superobjectives, inciting action, turning point, climax, and resolution. You will then arrange these cards in a specific order or layout to see the relationship between the individual parts and the whole.

This exercise may be done at any time in the genesis of a creative work. As a form of scenario building, it can be used to help put the pieces of a rough idea into some sort of order to see how things hang together. It can also be used as a method of analysis for a script in early drafts to see how the play is functioning. It may also be used to try out different ideas (a change of protagonist, an alternative inciting event, a different antagonist) to see how these changes might affect the play as a whole without having to write a whole draft. This analytical tool can also be used to provide the basis of a conversation between playwright and director and/or dramaturg. If each collaborator does his or her own version of this activity, it will clearly show whether or not each person is seeing the same play.

The one use that should *never* be made of this exercise is to consider it a formula, or a fill-in-the-blank activity for play construction. If certain elements are unknown, simply leave them blank. Sometimes it is as important to know what you don't know as it is to know what you know. The blank cards will teach you as much as those that are clear and specific. They will help you know where to go next and chart the territory that is still unknown.

The Cards

On nine individual slips of paper, draw or capture in words the following elements of your play:

1. *Protagonist*: Describe the external characteristics of your primary character or characters. This is the character or force at the center of your play. (Corresponds to the Significator in tarot.)

2. *World*: Describe the world or worlds of your play in terms of time and place, historical period, real or imaginary, single or multiple dimensions. (Corresponds to the Atmosphere in the tarot.)

3. *Antagonist*: Describe the opposing force and how it is revealed. This is the primary character or characters or forces creating the dramatic tension. (Corresponds to the Obstacle in the tarot.)

4. *Unconscious*: Describe the deeply buried feelings, fears, obsessions, and other psychological forces that inhibit or hold the protagonist back. These are internal forces that the protagonist may or may not realize are at work. (Corresponds to the Root in the tarot.)

5. *Superobjective*: Describe the protagonist's primary motivation or objective. What does he or she want or think he or she wants more than anything? This is usually an external goal. (Corresponds to General Sky in the tarot.)

6. *Inciting Event*: Describe the event that happens to upset the balance of the status quo and to kick off the dramatic action. (Corresponds to the Recent Past in the tarot.)

7. *Rising Action*: List as many of the events of the play as you know at this time. (Corresponds to Immediate Future in the tarot.)

8. *Climax*: Describe the turning point of the action, which brings the previous action to a head and triggers a reversal of some kind. (Corresponds to the Turning Point in the tarot.)

9. *Resolution*: Describe the new state of balance at the end of the play. (Corresponds to the Outcome in the tarot.)

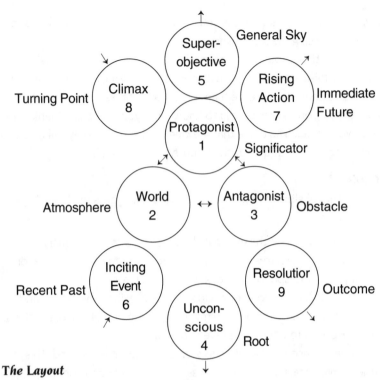

The Layout

Place your cards in this order on a large, flat surface. This layout is designed to show the interrelationship of parts of a dramatic action. It can be used to help you see at a glance if the parts are in the right kind of alignment to produce dramatic tension. A play is more than the sum of its parts, and a dramatic action is the result of the tension that exists between those parts.

1. Look at what you have written on cards 1, 2, and 3.

The inner triangle of cards 1, 2, and 3 describes the primary conflict of the play. The tensional relationship that exists between the protagonist, the world and the antagonist or antagonistic force generates the primary conflict that fuels the action. If there is no tensional relationship here, you might want to consider whether or not you have identified the correct character as the protagonist or if you need to intensify your antagonistic force.

2. Now look at the relationship between cards 1,4, and 5 to see the spine of conflict within the protagonist.

The internal conflict within the protagonist is depicted by looking at the relationship between 1, 4, and 5 as they illustrate how the conscious desires and motivations of the protagonist are often in conflict with the unconscious forces that inhibit or restrain the character. If there is no tensional relationship here, you might want to give a bit more thought to either the character's objectives or his or her unconscious inhibitions.

3. The relationship between cards 6, 2, 1, and 7 shows how the inciting action causes a chain reaction between the protagonist and his or her world, leading to the events of the rising action.

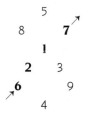

If there is no connection between the cause and effect of these events, you may want to consider upping the stakes or finding a different kind of connection not based on linear connections (e.g., thematic connections of image to image). Usually, the velocity of rising action builds suspense and momentum.

4. The interaction between cards 1, 7, 5, and 8 shows how the dramatic action builds to a climax as the need intensifies for the protagonist to achieve the superobjective.

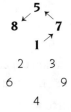

If there is no connection between the primary motivation or objective of the protagonist and the climax of the play, this might indicate a more passive protagonist than you want. These cards might also help you determine if the climax happens in the right place to trigger the falling action of the play.

5. The downward diagonal vector 8, 1, 3, and 9 indicates how the climax causes the final and ultimate confrontation between the protagonist and the antagonist and results in some action that brings about the resolution of the play.

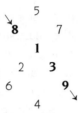

The velocity of falling action keeps the momentum going and does not allow it to stall before conclusion. Is the outcome the inevitable result of all that has gone before, or does it come out of nowhere?

6. Look again at the entire chart to see the overall patterns of your choices.

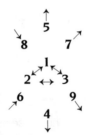

The strength of the conflict can be seen in the degree of tension between 1, 2, and 3.

The inner conflict of the protagonist is reflected in the interplay of 4, 1, and 5.

The velocity of the rising action is indicated in the intensity of the tension between 6, 2, 1, and 7.

The climax and reversal are driven by the chain of events motivated by the need of the protagonist to achieve the objective, as seen in the interaction between 1, 7, 5, and 8.

The inevitability of the resolution depends upon the collision course set up by the interaction of 8, 1, 3, and 9.

7. Is this the play you intended to write?

Creating a Monomyth

This exercise may be done individually or with a group in a class or work-shop. If it is done in a group, individual participants can each add an element to a group monomyth and assemble the final result as a collaborative activity.

If done as a solo exercise, you may use the raw materials of a play you are working on or you may start from scratch. If you use a play in progress, take the characters and events you have already created and imagine them in mythic terms. Try to see your protagonist as an archetypal hero on some kind of quest, be it internal or external. Are there other characters who might fill the functions of the old god, crone, goddess, or the one who gives super-natural aid? Are there plot elements that correspond to the call, threshold, road of trials, apotheosis, return, and homecoming? If you decide to start from scratch, allow the elements and events indicated below to suggest bold images born of archetypes. This activity will give you the opportunity to tell this tale in either written or visual form or both.

Clustering (from Campbell)

Divide a large piece of paper into six blocks or squares or use six separate sheets of paper.

In the center of each square write the following words:

Hero

The Call

Threshold

Road of Trials

Apotheosis

Homecoming

Take a moment to review the meaning of each of these terms as taken from Joseph Campbell's description of the monomyth on pages 104–105.

Allow the parts of the monomyth to suggest images and ideas freely.

Don't worry about how they might fit together; just brainstorm.

After you have clustered all six terms, put them aside for the moment and switch to the medium of drawing.

Monomyth Murals

Divide a large piece of paper into four quadrants. Label each section with the following words. Take a moment to consider what each of these words means to you and the forces in your play.

Monsters: Darkness, giants, wicked witches: make them as terrifying as you dare.

Mentors: Teachers, therapists, parents: give them all powers beyond the limits of human possibility.

Weapons: Amulets, charms, potions, swords, talents, abilities: things your hero possesses or can do that make her or him powerful.

Wounds: Vulnerabilities or limitations your hero faces: physical, psychological, or practical.

In each quadrant, draw or sketch images for each of these elements. Use analog drawings, symbols, or pictures to express your ideas.

Draw an epic mural of a great adventure that combines the images you just created.

Multiple times and places can be represented simultaneously.

Do not plan this in advance; allow it to unfold in the act of drawing.

How the drawing looks is much less important than what it teaches.

Writing the Monomyth

Using both the drawing and the clusters as guides, create a monomyth, first in narrative form and then in dramatic form as either a play or a screenplay. If this activity is done in a group, the monomyth can be written as a round-robin, where one member starts and the others add on, or as a collaboration working from consensus.

A WORD OR TWO . . .

Dealing with issues of sacred space can be a delicate business. A person's spiritual beliefs are often deeply held and intensely private. While some people will automatically connect what is sacred in their lives to an organized religion with established doctrines, others will reject this notion and find their worship in a shaft of sunlight or a quiet moment. In sacred space, there is always a sense of immensity, an expansion of thought and being into something older, larger, and wiser than ourselves.

In the exploration of sacred space, we should look first to the mythic elements of our own lives. Each of us has had the benefit of supernatural aid from a mentor or guide. Most of us have crossed thresholds into dimensions that seemed to take us out of the everyday into the underworld. We have all had our roads of trials. What transforms an experience from something ordinary into something sacred is the artist's ability to see the mythic dimension in what seems commonplace, to articulate the archetype, and to illuminate the universal within the specific. When this occurs, the invisible is made visible and the theatre is, once again, a sacred space.

NOTES

1. Peter Brook, *The Empty Space* (New York: Touchstone, 1995), 21.

2. Mircea Eliade, *The Sacred and Profane: The Nature of Religion*, trans. William R. Trask (New York: Harper, 1959), 22.

3. Yi-Fu Tuan, *Space and Place: The Perspective of Experience* (Minneapolis: University of Minnesota Press, 1977), 88.

4. Eliade, *The Sacred and Profane*, 53.

5. Carl Jung, *Man and His Symbols* (New York: Dell, 1977), 174.

6. Naomi Iizuka, "What Myths May Come," *American Theatre Magazine* (Sept. 1999): 18.

7. Joseph Campbell, *The Hero with a Thousand Faces* (Princeton, NJ: Princeton University Press, 1973), 30.

8. Jean Houston, *The Possible Human: A Course in Enhancing Your Physical, Mental, and Creative Abilities* (Los Angeles: J. P. Tarcher, 1982), 16.

9. Ibid., 16–17.

10. For more information on the Motherpeace Tarot, see *Motherpeace: A Way to the Goddess Through Myth, Art, and Tarot*, by Vicki Noble (San Francisco: HarperSanFrancisco, 1994).

7

CHAPTER

Dream Space

IN THE DREAMTIME, ABORIGINAL TRIBESMEN DEFINED SPACE AND established ownership of land by walking labyrinthine songlines, invisible pathways that meandered all over the continent of Australia. As they walked, they reenacted a creation myth that told of ancient beings wandering over the earth, singing out the names of everything that crossed their path: animals, plants, rocks, water. These ancient ancestors scattered a trail of words and notes in their footprints as they literally sang the world into existence.[1] The Dreamtime is a time out of time, a magical temporality where the powers of the world speak and listen in a common language. The land is part of the dreaming. It is the place from which life comes, the place where each person most belongs, where he finds his essence, where she creates her deepest self. The Dreamtime is not relegated to sleep; it is a constant state of awareness where the borders that separate past and present, conscious and unconscious are easily crossed.

There is another kind of dreamtime that exists for each of us on the other side of our eyelids every time we go to sleep. Whether we remember them or not, whether we acknowledge their power and presence in our lives or dismiss them out of hand, our dreams give us back all we have ever experienced or thought or feared or wondered about in fractured images and fleeting feelings. They connect each of us to our ancestors in the archetypes and mythic motifs of the collective unconscious. Dreams have fueled the creative processes of painters, filmmakers, poets, composers, choreographers, and playwrights. In both their form and their content, they have much to teach us about our waking world and about our secret selves.

Research indicates that all mammals dream, except perhaps dolphins and some species of seals.[2] Most of us spend approximately one-third of our lives in sleep and a large percentage of that time in dreams. During sleep our physical bodies go through a miraculous balancing act of restoration and repair. Hormones are secreted, replenishing the chemical balance of the endocrine system. Brain functions switch to an entirely different mode, processing information gathered during the day, storing images and emotions in specific sections of the brain. The experiences of our waking world are gathered up, sorted, and filed away for safekeeping in mind and muscle memory.

Dream space has inspired works of art in all disciplines, from the surrealistic paintings of Salvador Dali and René Magritte, to the imagistic films of Ingmar Bergman, Federico Fellini, and Robert Altman, to the interdisciplinary, postmodern theatrical experiments of Robert Wilson, Pina Bausch, Ping Chong, and Mary Zimmerman. The work of these artists has contributed to a popular conception of the nature of dreams. We understand and appreciate dreaming more fully because we have experienced their dreamlike visions. We appreciate the paintings of Salvador Dali as we look through the lenses of dreams and we look at dreams through the lenses of Dali. Perhaps more than any of the other spaces explored thus far in this book, dream space is a particularly foreign land with its own topography, geography, laws of physics, and concepts of time. Yet it is made entirely of our own thoughts, feelings, and memories.

DREAMING AND CREATIVE PROCESS

It supposedly happened on an afternoon in April 1797. Samuel Taylor Coleridge was dozing in a chair, lulled into a sleepy haze by a drop or two of laudanum, prescribed for a toothache. In his lap was a folio, *Purchas His Pilgrimage*, an account of exotic explorations. Just as he came to a sentence describing the palace and gardens of the mighty Asian potentate Kubla Khan, Colerige fell into a profound sleep and dreamed for about three hours. According to Coleridge's notebooks, he dreamed a poem in its entirety, about 250 to 300 lines. Upon waking, the poem still lingered in his mind in vibrant detail, not just as images and sensations, but in whole lines and stanzas of verse. Writing with a feverish intensity, he managed to scribble down only fifty-four lines before an unexpected visitor interrupted him. When he returned an hour or so later, the poem was gone, slipped from his mind and memory "like images on the surface of a stream into which a stone has been cast."[3]

There are other famous anecdotal examples of the impact of dreams on the writer's process. Mary Shelley claimed to have received the inspiration for her novel *Frankenstein* in an acute mental vision from a dream. Robert Louis Stevenson attributed many of his works to dreams, including a vision of Dr. Jekyll transforming into Mr. Hyde, glimpsed in the reflection of a window. Whether or not entire literary works have been composed in dreams is a matter of conjecture. Some scholars and scientists dismiss these anecdotal accounts as literary fabrications. John Livingston Lowes' *The Road to Xanadu: A Study in the Ways of the Imagination* (1964) traces the process of Coleridge's creation of both "Kubla Khan" and "The Rime of the Ancient Mariner" to original source material recorded in Coleridge's journals and diaries. Lowes contends that Coleridge stored mental pictures, words, and even phrases in his memory and that the drug-induced dream triggered a spontaneous creative combustion resulting in the poem, a confluence of images harvested from Coleridge's waking experience and the unconscious working of his creative genius. Whether the dream state produces or merely unlocks artistic impulses and ideas is irrelevant. There can be little doubt that creative synthesis is both a conscious and an unconscious process that takes place in both waking and sleeping states.

In her poetic and inspirational book *Three Steps on the Ladder of Writing*, French writer and essayist Hélène Cixous states that writers must go to the School of Dreams: "We have to travel to the heart of the unconscious . . . but for this we have to walk, to use our whole body for the world to be made flesh exactly as this happens in our dreams."[4] Her words echo the songlines of the ancient Aboriginals. "One must go on foot, with the body. One has to go away, leave the self . . . one must walk as far as the night. One's own night, walking through the self toward the dark."[5]

According to Cixous, dreams teach us how to write in four lessons:

1. They take us to other worlds without transition. We simply arrive without passport or introductions.
2. They allow us to travel with great speed, which we cannot do in life.
3. The dream says something that is never said, that will never be said by anyone else.
4. Dreams remind us of the mysteries we have lost. If we have lost everything in reality, dreams enable us to restore those moments when we are greatest, strongest in strength and in weakness—when we are magic.[6]

In these four simple lessons, Cixous summarizes the gifts that dreams have to give us as playwrights. The ability to move freely and quickly between dimensions of fantasy and reality, past and present, logic and illogic in a surreal world where anything is possible is a hallmark of both dream space and much experimental theatre. In dreams, territories and boundaries between dimensions of perception are fluid and ever changing. This has as much to do with the structure and interior logic of the dream's composition as it does with the symbolic and archetypal content the dream presents. Many nontraditional plays and performance art pieces are similarly unbounded by linear concepts of time and space. In dreams, emotional states are intensified, sensory images are heightened, and there is a constant sensation of movement, unimpeded by possibility. Meaning in dreams is found beneath the surface of their structures, just as meaning is constructed in the mind of the audience and different spectators may come away from a performance with very different perceptions of the multiple meanings suggested by a play or piece of performance art.

THE FUNCTION AND MEANING OF DREAMS: MULTIPLE PERSPECTIVES

Psychotherapists, psychoanalysts, and "dream workers" generally hold the view that the function of dreams is to express or reveal our deepest thoughts, feelings, desires, and needs. Dreaming is deep thought. From the beginning of the twentieth century to the present day, dreams and their interpretation have formed the cornerstone of psychoanalytic theory, starting with Sigmund Freud, who believed that dreams were indicators of psychic disturbance buried deep within the unconscious. According to Freud, all dreams are symbolic and most symbols are indicative of deeply repressed sexual desires. Carl Jung provides a different view of dreams and their importance to artists. Rejecting Freud's insistence that the life energy is primarily sexual and pathological, Jung sought a higher spiritual plane and deeper layers of meaning in the messages of dreams. Jung discovered common patterns and motifs in dreams that are also found in myths, legends, religious rituals, and practices from diverse cultures around the world. Some dreams contain archetypal figures and forces that Jung believed could not have come solely from the dreamer's personal experience. From this, he concluded that beneath the conscious mind of the waking state and the personal unconscious lies a third level, a deeper kind of knowing that resides within every human being. He called this level the collective unconscious. Dream figures belonging to the collective unconscious are made manifest in archetypes. Dreams provide a gateway into the mythic world and allow the dreamer to reconnect with an ancient sense of self, not unlike the Aboriginal walking the songline in communion with his ancestors.

Many contemporary psychologists take less theoretical, more practical approaches to dream work, such as Frederic "Fritz" Perls, founder of Gestalt therapy. To Perls, dream elements are not symbols needing interpretation, nor are they archetypal incarnations of ancient impulses. They are, quite simply, aspects of the dreamer's personality and reflections of his or her present circumstances. The dream is not something that happens to the dreamer as a passive spectator; it is an active process in which the dreamer receives information about the waking world and uses this information to change his or her behavior in direct and tangible ways.

Not everyone in the scientific community agrees with the notion that dreams reveal encoded facets of the human personality. There are those who believe that dreams are simply white noise caused by physiological functions of the brain and endocrine system that take place during sleep. Like a computer disc that has been scrambled so that bits and pieces of information turn up in random order and out of any logical sequence, the dreaming mind is filled with chatter, or static, projected onto the television screen of the unconscious. This somewhat unglamorous assessment seems to contradict the deeply held belief that dreams are somehow a key to the inner resources of the subconscious world. All dreams are not equally potent; many, if not most, are forgotten immediately upon waking. Vivid dreams that remain with us for hours or days or even years, the dreams that Jung called "Grand Dreams," are relatively rare. Sleep research has indicated that different stages of sleep produce dreams that vary in intensity, imagery, and emotional velocity. The reasons for this are rooted firmly in physiology.

In his book *Dreaming Souls*, Owen Flanagan presents a clear synthesis of the stages we generally experience in sleep and the kinds of dreaming that take place in each of them. Each stage is measured by changes in brain-wave activity and labeled with the letters of the Greek alphabet.[7] When we are awake and alert, our brains exhibit mostly beta brain waves, but as we become drowsy and start to drift off, brain waves cycle to a slower rate and produce alpha waves. This presleep state is akin to deep meditation and sometimes triggers fleeting visions and strange images, often of great beauty. This period is similar to lucid dreaming, when the dreamer is functionally asleep but is aware that he or she is dreaming. The lucid state is particularly rich for artists and writers. The conscious mind frets and fiddles and puzzles and posits questions and concerns while the unconscious mind offers solutions in strange and wondrous forms. A great deal of creative problem solving takes place in this netherworld between sleep and waking. Best of all, these images and ideas are often remembered in the morning!

As we descend deeper into sleep, our bodies relax, and alpha waves give way to theta waves, which have an even lower frequency. Eventually, delta waves take over, indicating deep sleep, and we move fully into the domain of the unconscious. Dreams during this period are often connected to worries and concerns of the wakeful world that repeat over and over. They are often accompanied by feelings of frustration, of running in place, of moving without actually getting anywhere.

After we have cycled through all four stages of sleep, something extraordinary happens: we move into REM sleep, characterized by rapid eye movement. The eyes seem to be tracking images, following unseen objects in motion. Brain waves experience a rapid rise back through all four stages in reverse order: delta, theta, alpha, beta! Heart rates increase and begin a period of wild fluctuation. Respiration grows alternately deeper and more shallow. Temperature rises and then drops. Secretion of sex hormones can trigger arousal. On an electroencephalograph measuring brain-wave activity, this kind of sleep looks more like a waking state than sleep. The body seems to be responding to external events, but the stimulus is actually coming from within the dreamer. REM dreams are quite different from those produced by non-REM sleep. Sensory perceptions are sharpened, resulting in the experience of sight, smell, taste, and physical sensations of walking, running, and flying. Emotional responses are intensified; visual imagery is vivid and clear, if often bizarre and illogical. The physiological response to REM dreaming is almost as if the events in our dreams were really happening, but the stimulus is entirely caused by neurons firing in the brain stem. Luckily, the body protects us with a drop in muscle tonus and decreased spinal activity, which results in a temporary paralysis that prevents us from getting up out of bed and fleeing the monster or leaping from windows to fly. These are the dreams that are often most useful to the writer, for they are expressed in psychophysical sensations, often with great emotional intensity. They assume a kind of narrative flow that defies conventional logic, as the brain tries to organize the onslaught of electrochemical impulses into some kind of order. Like an overworked dramaturg, the brain creates story out of chaos as a physiological function of sleep.

DREAM STRUCTURE AND LOGIC

When working with dreams, it is useful for playwrights to look beyond the dreams' content and symbols to see what they have to teach about nonlinear structures and interior logic. The various ways that dreams organize themselves in a kind of disordered order, the speed or slowness of their movement from image to image and event to event, and their ability to transform people, places, and events instantaneously all contribute to a narrative structure that seems to have no structure. If we look more deeply below the surface, there are some basic commonalities that bear a striking resemblance to the ways experimental writers have played with form and structure in many contemporary, and not so contemporary, plays.

In Freud's analysis of hundreds of dreams, he pointed out that dream events seem to be connected in four different patterns:

Simultaneity: Two or more events happen at the same time

Contiguity: Events follow one another sequentially

Transformation: One thing turns into another thing

Similarity: One thing or event resembles another

Virtually all of these connectors of disconnected material can also be found in plays with nonlinear structures, from Strindberg's *Dream Play*, to Mac Wellman's *Bad Penny*, to Suzan-Lori Parks' *Imperceptible Mutabilities In The Third Kingdom*. In the traditional, so-called well-made play, events are usually linked by contiguity, where one event follows another in a relationship of cause and effect or chronology. Dream logic, however, provides some interesting alternatives to these straightforward connections. In *New Playwriting Strategies*, Paul Castagno describes several variations on the open-ended episodic structures found in many language-based experimental plays that correspond rather neatly to Freud's terminology.

Serial Episodic Approach: The progression of scenes builds toward a climax or major point of complication. (contiguity)

Parallel Episodic Approach: Succeeding scenes disclose separate story units, but at some point the stories converge or the characters intertwine. (similarity)

Nonserial Juxtaposition: Scenes are juxtaposed and individual scenes are repeated with variation. A strong thematic thread holds together the disparate scenes. (simultaneity and transformation)[8]

Heather MacDonald's lyrical play *The Rivers and Ravines* provides an excellent example of simultaneity. The play deals with the struggles townspeople in a rural Colorado community go through while desperately trying to hold onto their farms in the face of recession and bankruptcy. In the final scene a family gathers at Thanksgiving dinner, and at the same time, in the same space, a farm auction is taking place to sell off their farm equipment and personal possessions. The irony is heartbreaking as platters of food are passed from person to person, only to be swept up into the other reality of the bankruptcy sale and sold to the highest bidder. Arthur Kopit's *Wings* provides examples of both contiguity and similarity in the story of a woman who has suffered a devastating stroke. The opening, titled "The Catastrophe," is presented in three lists: one of sounds, one of images, and one made up of the words of the woman. The sequence of the stroke's onset is contiguous while the connections between the fragmented images of a shattering mind and the gradual loss of both speech and identity are achieved by similarities between the individual simultaneous beats. An excellent example of transformation can be found in Lisa D'Amour's contemporary fairy tale *Anna Bella Eema* in a scene where a policeman inquiring about a child's welfare transforms into a Frankenstein monster and then back again into the policeman.

DREAM NARRATIVE

On the surface, both dreams and nonlinear plays may seem to be somewhat chaotic, but in truth, there are organizing principles and demonstrable connections between elements that provide a sturdy framework, if we just know how to look. Once again, this is analogous to the physiological process of brain function during sleep.

Owen Flanagan presents a fascinating glimpse into how the sleeping mind creates narrative. According to Flanagan, the brain has a natural proclivity to make sense out of disparate pieces of information. While we are awake, our conscious mind handles incredible amounts of information every second. It keeps track of our external reality, monitoring our sensory perceptions and channeling responses to the appropriate parts of the body. It stores all our present experiences as memories and accesses past memories to help us identify people, things, and behaviors we already know. It forms conjectures about the future, allowing us to make plans and anticipate future events. It is the day job of the brain to make sense of everything presented to our conscious mind, but this ability does not turn off after sleep just because we are unconscious.

At night both our bodies and our brains are engaged in very different activities from the daylight hours, and they are very, very busy. The endocrine system adjusts and regulates all the chemical balances in the body. Adrenal glands replenish the supply of cortisol, which controls the metabolism. Neurochemicals that regulate mood, attention, and control of conscious memory are turned down. Melatonin is released, which makes us drowsy. In short, our body chemistry changes at night, which has an impact on our psychophysical experience. During sleep there is greater activation of emotional areas of the brain and fewer neurochemical inhibitors to regulate mood and feelings. Feelings are intensified; happiness becomes elation; anxiety becomes terror. Cognitive screens and censors are turned off or down while we sleep so that thoughts, images, ideas, feelings, and memories run relatively freely through our unconscious minds. The connections between these fragments are freed from the boundaries of logic, and the usual rules of propriety are flagrantly broken. Wildly inappropriate images run rampant without the consequences one might impose in the daylight hours. But while the party rages on, the brain cortex keeps trying to do its job, which is to organize information in some way that is useful, resulting in strange and disconnected narratives that have a kind of illogical logic and disordered order. The dreaming mind takes the random noise and attempts to generate a narrative, bit by bit, trying to make sense of dreams.[9] The cerebral cortex keeps trying to put all of the wild images, emotions, memories, thoughts, problems, ideas, fears, and fantasies we have ever experienced into some kind of order.

According to Flanagan, the need to create narrative is a physiological function of the brain embedded into our DNA. It is the way we organize experience and make sense of our lives. During the day our conscious mind presents one kind of narrative: a linear, logical progression of events, which results in a cohesive story. But at night, the unconscious allows a very different kind of processing. In the seeming chaos of dreamtime, significance and structure can be found as long as the dreamer is willing to look!

For the playwright, incorporating dreams into plays can be tricky. Dream scenes are notoriously difficult to write without seeming heavy-handed and overly interpretive. In its day the "Dream Ballet" from the Rogers and Hammerstein musical *Oklahoma!* was hailed as innovative and psychologically complex. Looking at the same scene from the 1955 movie version today suggests a slightly different perspective. While Agnes DeMille's choreography is beautiful and moves the story line forward, one can't help but smile at the all too obvious Freudian overtones of its symbolism, reinforced by the

Salvador Dali—esque scenic elements of staircases leading nowhere and fragmentary furniture. In plays, film, and television, dream scenes often feel like a bit of a cheat, as they reveal a character's psychological state. The problem is often that the access is too direct. Like a heavy-handed therapist, the writer has presented the interpretation of the dream instead of the dream itself.

Dreams are most effective when they are not identified as dreams, but exist as the seeming reality of the world of the play. A recent student of mine set a play in a surreal landscape that is alternately a contemporary grocery store and a mental institution. One is never sure which location is the operant reality, as characters move through highly choreographed sequences with shopping carts, intercut with scenes about procedures for hospitalization. By deftly blending and colliding the two worlds, the playwright made connections using simultaneity and transformation to constantly keep both her protagonist and her audience off balance.[10]

Another effective use of dream space is to create dreams for your characters that will never appear in the actual play. These can give you insight into psychological dimensions of your characters without the pitfall of overly interpretive symbolism. Characters reveal themselves one layer at a time and dreams can be one of the most direct yet indirect ways to access the hidden depth of their unconscious minds.

The following exercises are designed to give you a physical experience with the ways dreams connect events and elements and to provide some suggestions for using your own dreams and those of your characters in your work.

MOVEMENT: MULTITRACKING EXERCISE

In Jean Houston's *The Possible Human*, Jim and I found a movement activity that mirrors both the form and structure of dreams.[11] Houston's purpose was to demonstrate the ability of the conscious mind to work on many sensory and perceptual tracks simultaneously. This bears great similarity to dreams, where fragmented images, memories, sensations, times, and places coexist without contradiction. Follow these directions playfully and do not allow the multiple tracks of this experience to become frustrating. In dreams the impossible is possible.

To begin, stand up and make sure that you have enough room to move freely. Get centered and balanced.

Let your head and shoulders move from right to left together in an even swinging movement.

Now let your head and shoulders swing apart—that is, move your head and shoulders in opposite directions from each other, with your head going left while your shoulders go right, and your shoulders going left while your head goes to the right.

Now your head and shoulders swing together . . .

And apart . . .

Together . . .

And apart . . .

Now, with your head moving in the opposite direction from your shoulders, let your eyes follow the shoulders. It is rather like flirting!

Now return to just the head and shoulders moving in opposite directions; let your eyes do anything they like. At the same time, tap dance.

At the same time, sing a song like "Tea for Two."

Stop at the end of the song and rest for a minute.

Now let your head go right and your face go left.

Now reverse and let your head go left and your face go right.

Keep on doing this, reversing the order each time.

Add a little jog and snap your fingers. At the same time, move your hands in circles.

And hum "Yankee Doodle Dandy"!

And simultaneously think about a hive of bees, a spiral staircase, and a bowl of Jell-O!

Stop and rest for a moment.

Now let your hips and arms swing back and forth together.

Now let your hips and arms swing in opposite directions.

Now together again.

Now in opposite directions.

At the same time, jump up and down.

Add a boxing movement with your hands.

And whistle "Dixie."

And think about Marie Antoinette, a ski slope in the Alps, and a giraffe.

Add a giant traffic jam and buttered popcorn.

Stop and rest for a minute.

Lie down on your back on the floor with your knees bent, the soles of your feet on the ground, and your hands on your chest.

Begin to raise and lower your elbows in a flapping motion.

At the same time, bicycle with your legs.

Now put your feet on the ground and open your knees wide and bring them back together again in a flapping motion while you bicycle with your arms.

Now flap with your arms and bicycle with your legs.

Change.

Change once again.

Sing "Bicycle Built for Two," changing the motion with your arms and legs at the end of each line.

Stop and rest for a minute after you have done this for a while.

Still lying down with your knees bent and your arms at your sides, begin beating very slowly with your right hand.

Now add a fast beat with your left hand while your right hand continues to beat slowly.

Keeping these two motions going, let your right foot begin to tap a slow beat.

Keeping all these motions going, let your left foot begin to tap a fast beat.

Stop.

Let your left hand beat a slow beat.

Now add your right foot tapping a slow beat.

Now add your right hand beating a fast beat.

Now add your left foot tapping a fast beat. Keep all this going.

Stop and rest.

Stand up now and let your head go right and your face go left.

Now reverse and let your head go left and your face go right.

Keep on doing this, reversing the order each time.

Add a little jog and snap your fingers. At the same time, move your hands in circles.

And hum "Yankee Doodle Dandy"!

And simultaneously think about a hive of bees, a spiral staircase, and a bowl of Jell-O!

Stop and rest for a minute. Be aware of any improvements you have noticed.

You can repeat this exercise many times, adding different sensory and kinesthetic elements drawn directly from your dreams. The most important part of the exercise is to keep it moving quickly, with abrupt shifts in images and transitions that mirror the elements of dream logic: simultaneity, contiguity, transformation, and similarity.

DREAM SPACE EXERCISES

Dream Journal

Stop right there! Don't even say it! I know what you are thinking. How can I keep a dream journal when I never remember my dreams? When I first started working on these activities, I gave my students and myself the assignment to keep a dream journal for the whole semester. From that day on, I didn't remember a single dream. I would wake up in the morning aware that I had dreamed, but when I tried to remember the dream, my mind would go blank. It was only later that I realized that the sheer act of grabbing a notebook, finding a pen, and trying to write something down dried up whatever tiny scraps of the dream were still hanging out around the edges of my conscious mind. So the first instruction in this activity is

Don't keep a dream journal!
Actually, do keep a dream journal, but don't make it a regular journal kind of journal.

Keep a pad of newsprint or a bunch of index cards and some crayons, colored pencils, or markers beside your bed.

Place an expandable file folder with separate sections nearby.

In the morning after you have dreamed, before you do anything else, remember the dream in the language of the dream.

See visual images in as much detail as you can.

Reexperience all of the physical sensations and feelings.

Allow yourself to experience the events; play them over and over.

Don't try to remember the dream in sequence.

Collect your dreams in bits and pieces.

Take a minute to write a word or two on a card or sketch a picture.

Drop the dream fragment in the expandable file.

If the fragments spool out like a continuous narrative, that's fine, but do not try to impose an order that they do not have.

Dream Fragments

Once you decide to work with a dream, select several dream elements from your file. Be sure to include a variety of elements: visual images, words, sounds, and kinesthetic sensations and emotions. Before you construct the final form of the new dream from these basic building blocks, take a few moments to work with the individual elements to see what they may reveal. Do *not* try to interpret what the elements mean. Simply allow them to be. Avoid all generic guides to the interpretation of dream symbols; most of the time they are nonsense.

Gestalting

Pick one element of the dream: person, place, object, and so on.

Describe the element in the voice of the element in the first person: "I am . . ."

Pay attention to your physical being as that element.

Pay attention to your feelings as that element.

Choose another element in the dream: person, place, object, and so on.

Describe the element in the voice of the element in the first person: "I am . . ."

Pay attention to your physical being.

Pay attention to your feelings.

Create a dialogue between the two elements.

Is there a tensional relationship between them?

What is the source of that tension?

Intensify that tension.

Create a dialogue between yourself and one or both of the elements.

> Do the elements have a message for you?

> How do they express it?

Analog Drawing

Using a pencil, draw an analog response to each of the dream elements.

Use only the language of line: fast or slow, dark or light, smooth or jagged, broken or flowing.

Do not use any pictorial symbols of any kind.

Do not include any words.

How does the drawing correspond to any visual imagery generated by the dream?

Reexperiencing the Dream

After you have worked with the fragments in any way that seems to expand their vocabularies of images, events, and associations, take a nap and see if you can dream a new dream. If you are not sleepy, take a long run or a swim and let your mind take a little journey of its own.

Dream Weaving

Take any or all of the information, images, and feelings you have generated in your work with these fragments and weave a new dream. Remember that a dream creates its own structure as it goes along. Do not try to make linear or logical sense of it, as that will defy the interior logic of the dream. Allow the dream to take any form it chooses.

Character Dreams

Create a dream for one of the primary characters in one of your plays.

This dream might take place at any point in the action of the play or before the play starts or after it ends.

> Perhaps it is a childhood dream for an adult character.

> Perhaps it is a dream the character has when he or she is very old.

> Remember that this dream may never actually be part of the play. Its purpose is to be an exploratory tool for discovery.

Pick one element in the character's dream: person, place, object, and so on.

Describe the element in the voice of the element in the first person: "I am . . ."

Pay attention to the physical being of the element.

Pay attention to the feelings of the element.

Pay attention to all sensory elements of sound, smell, taste, and touch.

Choose another element in the dream: person, place, object, and so on.

Describe the element in the voice of the element in the first person: "I am . . ."

Pay attention to the physical being of the element.

Pay attention to the feelings of the element.

Pay attention to all sensory elements of sound, smell, taste, and touch.

Create a dialogue between the two elements.

Is there a tensional relationship between them?

What is the source of that tension?

Intensify that tension.

Create a dialogue between the character and one or both of the elements.

Do the elements have a message for the character?

How do they express it?

How does the character respond?

Weave a dream for your character.

Write or draw the dream in as much detail as you can.

Use the present tense as though the dream is happening now.

How does the information gleaned from the character's dream make itself manifest in the action of the play?

What does the dream have to teach you and your character?

A WORD OR TWO . . .

Our own dream space offers a rich and varied landscape for exploration. It is filled with every minute of our lives, all we have ever experienced or thought or felt or known, stored as memory. It holds our hopes and fears and plans for the future and puts us in touch with ancient mythic motifs and archetypes. The neurochemicals released in slumber allow us to experience the intense emotions and feelings of dreams in relative safety. The metaphoric transformations of dream images show us how to make connections between disparate pieces of ourselves with a logic beyond logic. Sleep provides the passageway to the dreamtime and allows each of us to travel our own songlines, singing the names of all we find into existence. Dreams come to us as gifts wrapped in bundles of sleep: they are ours to lose in forgetfulness, to cherish in self-knowledge, or to use in our work.

NOTES

1. Bruce Chatwin, *The Songlines* (New York: Penguin, 1987), 2.

2. Owen Flanagan, *Dreaming Souls: Sleep, Dreams, and the Evolution of the Conscious Mind* (New York: Oxford University Press, 2000).

3. Coleridge's notebooks, as quoted in John Livingston Lowes, *The Road to Xanadu: A Study in the Ways of the Imagination* (Boston: Houghton Mifflin, 1964), 325.

4. Hélène Cixous, *Three Steps on the Ladder of Writing* (New York: Columbia University Press, 1993), 65.

5. Ibid., 65.

6. Ibid., 79–90.

7. For further discussion of dream stages, see Flanagan, *Dreaming Souls*, 65–84.

8. Paul Castagno, *New Playwriting Strategies: A Language-Based Approach to Playwriting* (New York: Routledge, 2001), 121–22.

9. Flanagan, *Dreaming Souls*, 88–89, 127.

10. Kendal Lynch, *Aisle Seven* (Masters thesis play, University of Texas at Austin, 2005).

11. Jean Houston, *The Possible Human: A Course in Enhancing Your Physical, Mental, and Creative Abilities* (Los Angeles: J. P. Tarcher, 1982), 73–75.

CHAPTER

Geographical Space

Here I am, where I ought to be.
A writer must have a place where he or she feels this.
Location, whether it is to abandon it, or to draw it sharply,
is where we start.

—Louise Erdrich[1]

THE EXPLORATION OF A WRITER'S GEOGRAPHICAL SPACE IS A JOURNEY into a sense of place, a place of sense, a place where sense takes leave, or simply a place to leave. Because the act of live performance always happens in real time and real space, it always has a setting; it literally takes place somewhere. Whether it is a contemporary living room, a blasted heath, the Great Hole of History, or the chambers of a character's mind, the place of the play is in some way a manifestation of the writer's personal geography. In some cases this may be a reflection of the environment where the writer grew up, the childhood space where initial experiences of land and landscape, of family and community, of the pace, rhythm, and tempo of life were imprinted at an early age. For other writers, a sense of place is formed by the adult experiences of where they live and work, where they feel a sense of belonging and identity or dispossession and exclusion. A writer's ethnicity and sexual orientation also inform a sense of place, directly as a reflection of a specific cultural heritage, or indirectly in response to the experience of inclusion or marginalization in a dominant culture.

In a play or performance piece, a sense of place is evoked in many ways. Most obvious, of course, is in the physical setting, but place is also made manifest in characters—in their attitudes, their attributes, their losses and longings, their struggles and successes. Place is reflected in language

patterns: in the rhythm and cadence of dialogue, the length of sentences, figures of speech, colloquial uses of slang or profanity, fragments, phrases,
words, and sounds. Some playwrights are so strongly identified with a particular geographical region that it defines their work. Tennessee Williams,
Horton Foote, and Beth Henley are known as Southern writers, although all
three have set plays in times and places that defy this description. David
Mamet and Nicky Silver are generally identified as urban writers, an assump-
tion due as much to the rhythm and velocity of their language as to the settings of their plays. The ethnicities of Maria Irene Fornes, Jose Rivera, Phillip
Kan Gotanda, Alice Tuan, Ntozake Shange, and Suzan-Lori Parks inform their
work, from their conception of character and language, to style and tone, to
the political and sociological themes and motifs they inhabit and explore.
The same can be said for all writers. Our experiences of race, class, gender,
and personal history all contribute to our notions of geographical space.

Intimately connected to a sense of place are concepts of home and homeland, which are at once intensely personal and fiercely political. Home may be
a place from which one desperately tries to escape or a haven to which one
longs to return. Home is much more than the house where one lives: it is the
community that either embraces or excludes, the society that either accepts
or rejects, the nation that either embodies one's values and beliefs or betrays
those values with hypocrisy and empty promises. The tensional forces between belonging and exclusion, inclusion and marginalization, exile and
homecoming help the writer define character, determine plot, affect language,
and establish theme.

SENSE OF PLACE

The term *sense of place* is drawn from humanistic geography and refers to a lo-
cal structure of feeling. Place is defined not so much by the elements of topography as by the feelings and attachments that humans bring to a location
in past and present associations. For many people, their strongest connections are tied up with what they perceive to be their homeland. Geographer Yi-
Fu Tuan states, "Throughout time, human groups have tended to view their
homeland as the center of the world, the focal point of a cosmic structure."[2]
This center was not necessarily a specific place on the surface of Earth as
much as the conviction that values and beliefs could be attached to a location. "This profound attachment to the idea of homeland appears to be
worldwide and is not limited to any particular culture or economy. It is known

in literate and semi-literate cultures, to sedentary farmers, city dwellers and wandering nomads."[3] It might be assumed that in migratory societies constantly on the move, where land is occupied rather than owned, this tie to the land might be less intense. But just the opposite appears to be the case. A deep attachment to place is not so much a matter of land that belongs to people, but people who belong to the land. A place need not be particularly beautiful or easy to cultivate or inspiring or even welcoming, as long as it is home. In his essay "The Flatness," writer Michael Martone states:

> The flatness informs the writing of the Midwest. . . . And the way I feel about the Midwest is the way my skin feels, and the way I feel my own skin, in layers, and broad stripes and shades, in planes and in the periphery. It is the place of sense.[4]

FINDING YOUR SENSE OF PLACE

As an artist it is interesting to consider how geographical space affects your work. A sense of place can inform the choices you make about character, theme, language, plot, and even spectacle. It may be helpful to go back to the beginning and look for clues in your childhood. If you grew up in a rural community, chances are that you formed your early notions of size and dimension in relationship to the land. The fields surrounding your house, the vistas that stretched outside your window, the length of the rows that you planted and harvested, the height of the corn or the wheat were the measuring sticks that you used to form your notions of what is large, small, far, and near. The seasonal nature of planting, growing, and harvesting helped form your understanding of time. The emotional dynamics of weather—the joy of sun and rain, the depression of drought, the fear of an early frost—contributed to your feelings of safety and vulnerability. If you grew up in a large city, you had entirely different lessons. The pace and velocity of traffic, the sounds of horns and the air brakes of buses, and the constant coming and going of people on the sidewalk informed your sense of rhythm and tempo. Your neighbors on the other side of a shared wall in your apartment building gave you an appreciation or fear of others. The visibility of homeless people, the presence of crime, the possibility of danger made you diligent or diffident, callous or compassionate. These are the kinds of knowing that cannot be taught, only experienced. These are the kinds of knowing that you will reflect in your work.

Our earliest impressions of place affect us on both a conscious and an unconscious level. A recent student, whose plays are often set in abstract locations featuring multiple dimensions of time and place, revealed to the class that he was born prematurely and spent his earliest days in an incubator, hovering between life and death. Whether or not this experience actually affected his writing can never be known for sure, but on some level he believes that the time he spent between worlds may have affected his sense of place.

Many of us, myself included, grew up in a suburb, a place neither urban nor rural, combining elements of each but without the distinction of either environment. The whole idea of a suburb is sameness, a kind of bland illusion of equality. Large housing developments replace distinct neighborhoods and give the appearance of prosperity without the individuality of differing socioeconomic levels. No one is rich; no one is poor; everyone is just sort of the same. Regional distinctions become increasingly blurred by the proliferation of shopping malls. There is virtually no difference between a mall in Denver and one in Dallas or Duluth. They all have exactly the same stores, the same food courts, the same nonmusic music, the same escalators, fishponds, and artificial everything. They are hermetically sealed with an ecosystem of heating and cooling that erases the distinctions between seasons or regions or topography or time of day. From inside the mall, it could be noon or midnight, May or December, Alaska or Atlanta. It is difficult to find the individuality of place in geography these days. This presents the challenge of finding the unique quality of any particular place when our senses have been so desperately dulled in the sense of sameness.

On the other hand, novelist Louise Erdrich suggests that perhaps our common references to mass culture, to contemporary folk and sports heroes, even to brand names, provide a sense of community. "Whether we like it or not, we are bound together by that which may be cheapest and ugliest in our culture, but may also have an austere and resonant beauty in its economy of meaning. These symbols and heroes may annoy us, or comfort us, when we encounter them in literature; at the very least they give us context."[5] The key here is specificity. A sense of place, or of a person in a place, is created in the details. The character who drinks Schlitz is quite different from one who drinks Heineken. "Brand names and objects in fiction connote class, upbringing, aspirations, even regional background."[6] The need for detail and specificity is even more pressing in playwriting than in fiction. Without the luxury of narrative description, all aspects of geography must be embedded in theme, character, and action. A sense of place in playwriting must be found in the blood and bone of character and in the breath of language.

THE GEOGRAPHY OF LANGUAGE

A character's speech is like a fingerprint; it is unique and individual and it reveals its meaning indirectly. On paper, a fingerprint is a series of swirling lines and creases arranged in whorls, meaningless in and of themselves. The key to identity lies in patterns. And so it is with words. The words a character uses can reveal age, socioeconomic status, level of education, mental and emotional health, and, of course, his or her sense of place, right down to the city or perhaps even the neighborhood. A character's vocabulary provides the basic building blocks of identity in colloquialisms, slang expressions, figures of speech, and even the character's use of profanity. The pattern of words arranged in fragments or phrases or lines of dialogue often reveals more about a character than what he or she actually says. The length of lines, the use of phrases, and finished or unfinished sentences all indicate the nature of a character's thought and intensity of feeling. The rhythm of a character's speech and the counterpoint of dialogue provide a scene with its heartbeat. Interruptions can jump-start a sentence or derail a speech from its original intention. Repetition can increase emphasis or drain the energy out of an intention as it dwindles into meandering. The use of silence is often more powerful than words. What a character struggles to say and cannot articulate is more revealing than speech, for it allows the audience to fill in the words too personal or painful or passionate to say aloud.

In David Mamet's *Glengarry Glen Ross*, the language evokes urban Midwest with short, choppy phrases, explosive energy, incomplete thoughts, blunt use of profanity, and repetition like a jackhammer. The energy here is aggressively masculine, quick, direct, and heavy. Although a reader unfamiliar with the play might not understand at first that the speakers are talking about real estate, the city rhythm is unmistakable.

WILLIAMSON

Shelly, you blew the last . . .

LEVENE

No. John. No. Let's wait; let's back up here. I did . . . will you please? Wait a second. Please. I didn't "blow them." No. I didn't "blow" them. No. One kicked *out*, one I closed . . .

WILLIAMSON

. . . you didn't close. . .

LEVENE

. . . I, if you'd *listen* to me. Please. I *closed* the cocksucker. His *ex*. John, his *ex*, I didn't know he was married. . . he, the *judge* invalidated the . . .

WILLIAMSON

Shelly . . . [7]

The urban feeling of Mamet's language comes from every element of syntax: vocabulary, sentence structure, punctuation, and even the sounds of the words. The repetition of harsh plosives and guttural sounds in the words, *blow, please, closed, kicked,* and *cocksucker,* combined with incomplete and shattered sentences, propels the speed of the lines' delivery.

In contrast, the languid pace, lyrical, poetic imagery, and seductive rhythms of New Orleans are unmistakable in Tennessee Williams' A *Streetcar Named Desire.* Blanche winds the young delivery man in a silken skein of words made of gossamer laced with steel. Here the energy is feminine, sustained, light, and indirect. The language is sensuously Southern.

BLANCHE

Uh—What time is it?

YOUNG MAN

Fifteen of seven, ma'am.

BLANCHE

So late? Don't you just love these long rainy afternoons in New Orleans when an hour isn't just an hour—but a little piece of eternity dropped in your hands—and who knows what to do with it?

    (*She touches his shoulder*)

You—uh—didn't get wet in this rain?

YOUNG MAN

No ma'am, I stepped inside.

BLANCHE

In a drug store? And had a soda?

YOUNG MAN

Uh—Huh.

                    BLANCHE
Chocolate?

                    YOUNG MAN
No, ma'am. Cherry.

                    BLANCHE
Cherry!

                    YOUNG MAN
A cherry soda.

                    BLANCHE
You make my mouth water.[8]

Contrast the staccato rhythms of Mamet with the sensuous sounds Williams places in Blanche's mouth: *love, long, hour, eternity, soda, mouth, water.* The repetition of the word *cherry* works on many levels as a seduction, a sensory image, and a symbol of sexual innocence. The length of Blanche's sentences and the way she winds around to the point, tempting the boy with *chocolate* and *cherry* before she kisses him at the end of the scene, give the language a sustained feeling of lightness that is deceptively indirect but actually moves right to the point of physical contact. Both plays are blessed with very specific geographical locations reflected in character and language, but what of plays where the location is more abstract and metaphysical?

Suzan-Lori Parks' *The America Play* is set in "A Great Hole. In the middle of nowhere." The hole is an exact replica of the Great Hole of History, a theme park inhabited by dead American heroes. In this place, a black man known as Foundling Father, dressed as Abraham Lincoln, repeatedly plays out the assassination of Lincoln. Over and over he is shot by patrons who pay a penny for the privilege. In this play, Parks invents a new historiography, blending American myth and African American language traditions set in the dark heart of American violence.

(A *gunshot echoes. Loudly. And echoes.*)
LUCY: Hear that?
BRAZIL: Zit him?
LUCY: No.
BRAZIL: Oh.
(A *gunshot echoes. Loudly. And echoes.*)

LUCY: Hear?

BRAZIL: Zit him?

LUCY: Nope. Ssuhecho

BRAZIL: Ssuhecho

LUCY: UH ECHO UH HUHN. Of gunplay. Once upon uh time somebody
    had uh little gunplay and now thuh gun goes on playing: KER-BANG!
    KERBANG- kerbang-kerbang- (kerbang) – ((kerbang)).

BRAZIL: Thuh echoes

    (*Rest*)

    (*Rest*)

LUCY: You're stopped?

BRAZIL: Mmlistenin.[9]

Parks' dialogue reads like poetry, with stage directions as much a part of
the rhythm and flow of language as speech. She scores the scene like music,
using the term *rest* to indicate a pause, in this case two consecutive pauses.
Even the placement of words on the page is deliberate, with liberal use of
white space to indicate breath and cadence. Sentences are short and direct,
but without the explosive energy and anger in *Glengarry Glen Ross*. Rhythms
are slower here but not as languid as in A *Streetcar Named Desire*. In the speech
patterns of Lucy and Brazil, the plosives and hard C sounds slide into softer
Zs and Shhhhs. The repetition of the *uh* also softens the quality of the
speech, which is suddenly shattered by the explosive *kerbang* that echoes
into the distance.

    Although the Great Hole of History is not a literal geographical location,
Parks establishes a sense of place in the incongruity of the words and actions, the use of repetition as reverberation, unorthodox punctuation, and
the ways that words and symbols appear on the page. As gunshots echo
through time, Parks clearly indicates the way their sound diminishes in the
usual appearance of words on the page: "KER-BANG! KERBANG- kerbang-
kerbang- (kerbang)–((kerbang))." This is a world of incongruity where violence
is both horrific and humorous without losing the edge of either extreme.

THE PLACE OF HOME

If a sense of place is as much a function of the feeling of belonging as it is a
matter of location, then, conversely, the experience of exclusion is an equally
powerful force. This is nowhere more evident than in the often paradoxical re-

lationship that people have with the place to which they ought to feel the most intense sense of belonging: home. In her book *Staging Place*, Una Chaudhuri points out that "the privileged setting of modern drama is the family home."[10] From the drawing rooms of Chekhov, Ibsen, and Shaw, to the crumbling verandas of Tennessee Williams, to the cold-water flats of John Osborn and Harold Pinter, to battered farmhouses of Sam Shepherd, the literal depiction of the family home has been the setting of much of twentieth-century realism. But the views of home expressed by these writers are deeply conflicted. Home is either a battleground or a refuge, depending on the point of view. The sisters of Chekhov's *Three Sisters* and Madame Ranevskya and her entourage in *The Cherry Orchard* struggle desperately against the forces of changing times to hold on to their estates and their identities. Home is the last vestige of a society already gone. In the memory of happier times, it is the only place where life makes sense and gives the illusion of security. But to Ibsen's Hedda Gabler and Nora Tessman, home is the prison that traps these women in the stultifying identities and claustrophobic relationships that threaten to suffocate them. For these ladies, escape from the toxicity of home, either through desertion or death, is the only option.

Chaudhuri coins the term *geopathology* to express the "painful politics of location. . . . In geopathological dramaturgy, every character, every relationship is defined by a problem with place."[11] According to Chaudhuri, this begins with a rupture between human beings and their natural environment and is compounded by societal forces that increasingly emphasize dislocation, fragmentation, and alienation. The desire for an idealized sense of belonging is constantly disappointed by the reality of the place as it is.[12] The tensional force between yearning and experience is played out over and over in a variety of strikingly similar scenarios. There are three broad themes that repeatedly play themselves out in modern drama's preoccupation with the politics of home: leaving home, the failed homecoming, and homelessness; all three are aspects of geopathology.

Plays dealing with one or more characters leaving home, or trying to leave home, are almost too numerous to mention. From the tragedy of Edmond Tyrone's inability to leave his dysfunctional family in *Long Day's Journey into Night* to the comedy of Neil Simon's *Brighton Beach Memoirs*, coming of age is often the painful process of disentangling from a physical location as well as the family ties that chafe and bind. In Marsha Norman's *Night Mother*, Jessie chooses suicide rather than remaining in the depressed state of her home in the company of her desperately loving mother. Even if one manages to physically leave home, true escape is often impossible, as Tom discovers in *The Glass Menagerie*. From the distance of an undisclosed future, Tom remembers the crippling claustrophobia of the St. Louis apartment where he left his mother and sister. Even though he has left physically, he will always be trapped in memory. Past and present collide in a sense of place that he carries with him and cannot escape no matter how far he wanders.

The failed homecoming is another familiar domestic trope. In this scenario, a character returns home after a long period of being away, only to find the family irreparably damaged or to wreak havoc upon those who have remained behind. Harold Pinter's *The Homecoming* and Sam Shepherd's *Buried Child* both deal with sons returning to their families after six years. Their arrivals trigger a string of events that reveal deeply repressed secrets and interpersonal dynamics that wind up destroying any illusion of family unity. In Tina Howe's *Painting Churches*, Mags Church returns to her childhood home to help her aging parents and discovers that she can't go home again, even with the best of intentions. Like the return of the hero in Joseph Campbell's monomyth, the problem with place is that either it has changed or it hasn't. The prodigal son or daughter must either abandon illusions about a past that probably never was or shred what is left of the fragile fabric of family.

The absence of home as experienced by characters who are homeless can be as dramatically compelling and psychologically revealing as any scenario of leaving or returning. Chaudhuri points to the famous example of Beckett's *Waiting for Godot* as a depiction of "a homelessness so radical that it has regularly seemed to symbolize a universal condition."[13] The homeless youngsters in Naomi Iizuka's *Polaroid Stories* are passionately proud of their transience and build temporary shelters physically and emotionally for each other in the trash under a highway. Sometimes the safety of home has been destroyed by an outside force or apocalyptic disaster, as in *Marisol*, by Jose Rivera. Homelessness is a place where the absence of home, the impossibility of home, forces characters to come to terms with themselves and each other in direct and powerful ways.

Just as homelessness is a manifestation of geopathology, the placelessness of much of postmodern theatre offers a slightly different sense of geographical space. Many contemporary plays seem to exist in geographical abstraction or to inhabit multiple times and places simultaneously. In Eric Overmeyer's *On the Verge: The Geography of Yearning*, three Victorian time travelers find themselves on a "pathway of light," where modern gadgets, toys, and junk dangle before them as though they are growing in the sky. Suzan-Lori Parks' *Imperceptible Mutabilities of the Third Kingdom* uses three different locations and times simultaneously in a single scene: a slave ship, a Civil War plantation, and a modern luxury condominium. Chaudhuri labels this "topographic" theatre, which "posits a new kind of placement, not in any one circumscribed and clearly defined place but in the crossroads, pathways and junctions between places. This suggests a kind of placelessness, not as the absence or erasure of place, but as the combination or layering, one on top of another, of many different places, many distinct orders of spatiality."[14]

Even in these multivocal, multilocational plays, the problem with place is still finding where one belongs. Plays that happen in the space of everywhere seem to offer the characters roaming their complicated terrains nowhere to rest. Plays set in the space of nowhere are often filled with characters seeking a place where they can feel a sense of identity. These are the nomads without tribes, without a connection to a physical or an emotional landscape they can truly call their own.

In working with concepts of geographical space, my students discovered, not surprisingly, that language and character speech are often the most direct indicators of a sense of place. But this connection goes far deeper than simply matters of syntax, sentence structure, dialect, or dialogue. Speech is most effective when it reinforces an overall metaphor for the location of the play as a whole. One recent student found that a sense of place became a vital aspect of a monologue in which a cowboy twirls a lariat as he spins the story of his life as if it were a river. In his use of open vowel sounds, the fluidity of his imagery, and the action of circling the rope round and round, the cowboy and the river become one. Place becomes character as character becomes place.[15]

In the same semester another student brought in scenes from an epic piece about Las Vegas. By using real and imagined characters, giving voice to inanimate objects such a slot machines, and juxtaposing events as diverse as the flash of an atomic bomb test and a never ending parade of showgirls, she captured the complexity and contradictions of the city with specificity and elegant economy. Place becomes plot as plot becomes place.[16] In both of these examples, the playwrights distilled the essence of their respective geographies and effectively infused those qualities into character, speech, and action to such an extent that the elements became inseparable.

In the exercises that follow, we shall take a rather roundabout route to explore essential qualities of expression by starting with qualities of movement and then expanding these concepts into the development of character and language. We'll also journey into your own geographical spaces by suggesting ways to help you find a sense of place in yourself and in your work!

MOVEMENT: EFFORT/SHAPE

The key to the depiction of geographical space is to distill an essence of a place and to express that essence in words, images, and actions. This often involves taking qualities that are quite abstract and making them concrete in tangible ways. In order to do this, it is helpful to have a vocabulary that can be used to analyze and explore essential qualities of expression, whether they are made manifest in language, movement, or the psychophysical dimensions of character. For many years, Jim and I have adapted techniques based on Rudolph Laban's concepts of Effort/Shape to provide both actors and writers with just such a vocabulary.[17]

Laban is best known as the creator of Labanotation, a system used to create a written record of choreography depicted in a set of specific symbols. Although the symbols of Labanotation establish patterns of movement in visual form, the symbols alone do not capture the feeling or quality of that motion. Laban distilled eight "Effort terms" to describe the expressive qualities of the ways bodies move in space. These terms describe the polarities or extremes of the primary components of all movement: time (quick/sustained), weight (heavy/light), and space (direct/indirect). The eight words, or Efforts, that Laban formulated—*press, punch, dab, flick, slash, wring, float, glide*—describe the quickness or slowness, the heaviness or lightness, the directness or indirectness of movement. These words describe the quality of the movement, or how the movement is done. A long diagonal cross from one side of a room to another will be very different if it is done as a *float* than if it is done as a *slash*. The physical gesture of a *punch* is entirely different from that of a *flick*, although both might involve a sudden forward motion of the arm.

Experiencing the Efforts

The best way to learn about the qualities of Effort/Shape is to experience them. So we will begin with a sequence of movements that will literally get these words into your muscles and allow you to feel what they mean before you start wondering how they can be used.

Find a comfortable space to stand with plenty of room around you.

Imagine that you are pressing against a very heavy door with both your hands.

Now, physically *press* with all your strength.

Put your shoulder into it and use all your weight to *press*.

Now, say the word *press* and try to find as many ways of *pressing* with as many parts of your body as you can.

Keep saying the word *press*.

Physically move through space, *pressing* as you go.

Feel the *press* in all parts of your body.

Now, press a little more quickly, speed things up a bit, quicker still, until the movement changes and becomes:

punch.

Punch the air with your hands; shadow box.

Punch with your elbows, your knees, your shoulder, and your head.

Punch through space, moving across the floor, always *punching* as you move.

Punch with as many parts of your body as you can.

Keep saying the word *punch*.

Feel the *punch* in all parts of your body.

Now, punch a little more lightly, use less force, less weight, until the movement changes and becomes:

dab.

Dab at the air with your hands as if they are covered with paint.

Dab at the canvas of the room, the walls and the floor.

Dab imaginary calamine lotion all over yourself.

Keep saying the word *dab*.

Dab, *dab*, *dab*, with your elbows and knees.

Dab your way through the room, quickly, lightly, directly to the opposite wall.

Feel the *dab* in all parts of your body.

Now, dab with a little less directness, here and there, everywhere, until the movement changes and becomes:

flick.

Flick away an imaginary fly, a mosquito, a gnat.

Flick away a little dandruff from your shoulder.

Flick some fluff off the floor with your foot.

Keep saying the word *flick*.

Flick with your hands, your head, your eyelids.

Feel the *flick* in all parts of your body.

Now, flick with more weight, harder, heavier; use more strength until the movement changes and becomes:

slash.

Slash with your whole arm like a sword cutting through vines and underbrush.

Slash with both arms, cutting as you move.

Slash your way through a jungle, a swamp.

Slash with your arms and legs and torso.

Keep saying the word *slash*.

Slash with every part of your body.

Feel yourself *slashing* through space.

Now slash more slowly, slower still, in a slow sustained motion, until the movement changes and becomes:

wring.

Wring an imaginary washcloth in your hands.

Wring your arms in twisting knots.

Wring your stomach like a cramp in the gut.

Keep saying the word *wring*.

Wring your whole body in grief.

Feel the *wring* in every part of your body.

Now, wring more gently, use less force, lighter and lighter, until the movement becomes:

float.

Let your arms *float* above your head.

F*loat* with your head and neck, so light, so light.

Feel an imaginary wind blow you, here and there, and *float* all over the place.

F*loat* in your legs and feet as if you are walking on clouds.

Keep saying the word *float*.

F*loat* all over the room.

Feel the *float* all through your body.

Now, float toward a specific spot on the wall, move directly to it, until the movement becomes:

glide.

Glide across the floor as if you were ice-skating.

Glide through the air, like a glider on a glide path.

Glide with your arms full out like wings.

Glide to one place, then turn and *glide* directly to another.

Feel the *glide* in every part of your body.

STOP.

Effort Analysis

You have now experienced all eight of the effort states physically in your body, and as such, you have experienced the polarities of time, weight, and direction. As you moved from one effort to another, only one dimension of movement was changed at a time, which altered the quality of the movement to such an extent that it became a whole new effort. The polarities are as follows:

Time: quick or sustained

Weight: heavy or light

Space: direct or indirect

As you can see in the following tables, the eight effort terms represent the possible combinations of these polarities. The bold words indicate a change in polarity.

EFFORT	TIME	WEIGHT	SPACE
Press	sustained	heavy	direct
Punch	**quick**	heavy	direct
Dab	quick	**light**	direct
Flick	quick	light	**indirect**
Slash	quick	**heavy**	indirect
Wring	**sustained**	heavy	indirect
Float	sustained	**light**	indirect
Glide	sustained	light	**direct**

Application of the Efforts

Once you have experienced the differences in feeling between these eight qualities, you are in a position to apply this information in a number of ways. For example, an actor might use efforts to help find a physical life for a character, first by exaggerating these effort qualities into a character walk and then gradually replacing the exaggeration with more natural movements and gestures. A director might use the efforts as a sort of shorthand with actors to help them change the quality of a physical or vocal choice without resorting to generalities or judgments. As a playwright, use of these terms can help you define characters physically, kinesthetically, vocally, emotionally, and so on. They provide a natural link between language and movement. Think back for a moment on the three brief scenes discussed earlier in the chapter.

WILLIAMSON

Shelly, you blew the last . . .

LEVENE

No. John. No. Let's wait; let's back up here. I did… will you please? Wait a second. Please. I didn't "blow them." No. I didn't "blow" them. No. One kicked *out*, one I closed . . .

WILLIAMSON

. . .you didn't close . . .

LEVENE

. . .I, if you'd *listen* to me. Please. I *closed* the cocksucker. His *ex*. John, his *ex*, I didn't know he was married . . . he, the *judge* invalidated the . . .

WILLIAMSON

Shelly . . .

In Effort terms, Mamet's rapid-fire dialogue for Williamson is quick, heavy, and direct, a perfect example of *punch*. Since Levene's speech is also quick and heavy, but much less direct, his speech pattern is a *slash*. The dynamics of their argument build as they alternately *punch* and *slash* at each other. Their Efforts are similar but not identical. The seriousness of Levene's situation creates the weight in the scene and his urgency gives the scene its speed, but the difference in space (direct/indirect) provides contrast and variety.

Listen for the differences in the scene from A *Streetcar Named Desire*.

BLANCHE

Uh—What time is it?

YOUNG MAN

Fifteen of seven, ma'am.

BLANCHE

So late? Don't you just love these long rainy afternoons in New Orleans when an hour isn't just an hour—but a little piece of eternity dropped in your hands—and who knows what to do with it?

(*She touches his shoulder*)

You—uh—didn't get wet in this rain?

YOUNG MAN

No ma'am, I stepped inside.

BLANCHE

In a drug store? And had a soda?

YOUNG MAN

Uh—Huh.

BLANCHE

Chocolate?

YOUNG MAN

No, ma'am. Cherry.

BLANCHE

Cherry!

YOUNG MAN

A cherry soda.

BLANCHE

You make my mouth water.

As the Young Man attempts to answer Blanche's subtext-laden questions, his Effort qualities are light, quick, and direct (a *dab*) while Blanche's Effort qualities are far more sustained, light, and seemingly indirect at first (*float*), until she kisses him at the end of the scene (*glide*). The scene has an entirely different tempo, weight, and feeling from the staccato intensity of the Mamet dialogue; the differences are clearly seen in their Effort qualities.

The efforts in Suzan-Lori Parks' *The America Play* are a bit harder to identify, as the transcription of the vernacular really needs to be read aloud.

> (A *gunshot echoes. Loudly. And echoes.*)
> LUCY: Hear that?
> BRAZIL: Zit him?
> LUCY: No.
> BRAZIL: Oh.
> (A *gunshot echoes. Loudly. And echoes.*)
> LUCY: Hear?
> BRAZIL: Zit him?
> LUCY: Nope. Ssuhecho
> BRAZIL: Ssuhecho
> LUCY: UH ECHO UH HUHN. Of gunplay. Once upon uh time somebody
>   had uh little gunplay and now thuh gun goes on playing: KER-BANG!
>   KERBANG- kerbang-kerbang- (kerbang)–((kerbang)).
> BRAZIL: Thuh echoes
>   (*Rest*)
>   (*Rest*)
> LUCY: You're stopped?
> BRAZIL: Mmlistenin.

The initial exchanges between Brazil and Lucy are light, quick, and direct, a series of *dabs*, but the sound of the gunshot interrupts with a quick, heavy directness, a *punch*, that echoes and gradually diminishes back to the previous *dab*.

My analysis of these three scenes is highly subjective. Whether or not these qualities are a product of the geographical spaces these plays represent is somewhat speculative. The purpose of Effort analysis is intended to be evocative rather than limiting and to give writers, actors, and directors a way to play with choices to see how to most effectively convey the qualities of place and character they are trying to create.

Use of the Efforts is not limited to development of character and language. These terms can be helpful in finding variety in dynamics while building scenes. For example, if you are trying to write an argument between two characters and both are simply punching away at each other with quick, heavy, direct vocal jabs, the scene may become tedious and predictable. Consider for a moment an argument between a *slash* and a *float*. Although the *slash* has more weight and speed, the *float* is indirect and sustained. While the *slash* flails away, the *float* simply drifts past the blows. You can also apply these Effort terms to the way a scene progresses and changes in dynamics. This same hypothetical argument may start out with both characters *dabbing* and *flicking*, escalate into *punching* and *slashing*, and finally end with one character *wringing* in despair while the other *floats* away.

GEOGRAPHICAL SPACE EXERCISES

Effort qualities can also be seen in visual form in analog drawings. It is helpful to first get the Effort into your muscles by repeating and physicalizing the word and then drawing a response on a large piece of paper with a crayon or marker. By using different crayons, you will see if your response to the Effort has color as well as shape. For some people the more sustained Efforts with less weight, such as *float* and *glide*, are best represented with cooler colors, such as blue or green, while quicker Efforts with greater weight, such as *punch* and *slash*, suggest warmer colors like red and orange. It must be stressed, however, that these responses are very subjective. There is no right or wrong way to represent an Effort as long as the movement impulses accurately reflect the polarities of time, weight, and space. A problem occurs, however, when you intend one thing but do another. I have seen students scribbling with great force, drawing thick, heavy, jagged lines while saying "Float, float, float!" The word might be *float*, but their physical action and the drawing are *slashes*. As soon as they lighten the weight of their action, the Effort changes from *slash* to *float*.

Drawing and Writing with the Efforts

Sit on the floor with a box of crayons and eight pieces of blank paper.

Repeat the word *press* over and over to yourself.

Physicalize *press* in your muscles.

Pick up a crayon and draw your response to the experience of *press*.

Repeat the process with the other seven Effort terms: *punch, dab, flick, slash, wring, float,* and *glide*.

Compare the drawings to see how the elements of time, weight, and space are manifested visually.

Choose two drawings that are particularly evocative for you.

On separate pieces of paper, cluster each of the two Effort terms to see what words are suggested by each.

Using the drawings and clusters as source material, write a brief vignette or scene that incorporates both Efforts.

It may contain two characters each with a different Effort.

It may simply move in emotional dynamics from one Effort to the other.

The Efforts of Place

Visualize a geographical space that is particularly powerful for you.

This may be urban or rural; it may contain elements such as traffic, vehicles, animals, and so on, but it should *not* focus on people.

It would be helpful to have a visual image such as a photo or a painting to work from, but your imagination is also fine.

It is also helpful to imagine any sounds that might be in this place.

Attend to the time of this place. Is it quick and rhythmic or sustained and gentle?

Attend to the weight of this place. Is there a feeling of heaviness or lightness?

Attend to the use of space in this place. Are the compositional elements direct and focused or indirect and scattered?

Draw a quick analog drawing of the feeling of this place.

If the place had a voice, how would it speak?

Write a monologue in the voice of the place.

Which Effort terms are suggested by the place?

Write a brief vignette or a scene from a screenplay that deals *only* with the place (no people) in which one Effort quality changes into another Effort quality.

Finding a Sense of Place in Yourself

It is sometimes helpful to explore your own literal sense of place by starting with the literal geographic space where you formed your sense of self.

Write the name of what you consider to be your *hometown* on a piece
of paper.

This may be where you grew up as a child or an adult place.

This may be a place you loved or hated, a place that nurtured or
excluded you.

Answer the following prompts and questions just to prime your
memory bank.

Describe the land and how it affected you.

Describe the seasons and how they affected you.

What was the rhythm of this place?

What sounds, smells, and tastes do you remember?

Cluster the name of your hometown.

Write "Belong/Exclude" on a piece of paper.

Cluster "Belong/Exclude."

Write a brief vignette—a poem, story, dialogue, or monologue—that
incorporates some of the images and associations that came up for you in
the previous activities.

Finding a Sense of Place in Your Work

Think back over the plays, stories, and poems you have written.

Make a list of as many of the settings as you can remember.

Circle the titles of those pieces where place was particularly rich or
important. Cross out the titles of plays that might just as well have been
set in another time or geographic location.

Do the places of your plays reflect in any way your own personal sense of
place? How? Why?

Make a list of places you would like to explore in a play or story.

Write a scene or a play or a novel set in this place.

A WORD OR TWO . . .

When you discover a sense of place in your work, it is like coming home to
yourself. It is the place you have always lived, even though you may have
never been there before you wrote about it. The pulse of the place is your

heartbeat; the rhythm is your breath. It may be the literal place where you grew up, where you first formed your notions of the world around you. It may be some place quite different. It may be a different historical period; it may be on the other side of the world. You can read all about this place and this time. You can do research until it begins to feel like truth, but until you dwell in this place in the fullness of your imagination, until you walk the land, breathe the air, and put your whole body in this place, you will not really know it; you're just guessing. The characters who dwell in this place know it better than you do, but they will teach you all about it if you listen to them. When you find this sense of place in your writing, you may think that you have created it in your words and images and ideas. But in truth, it is quite the opposite. It is the sense of place that creates you!

NOTES

1. Louise Erdrich, "A Writer's Sense of Place," A *Place of Sense*, ed. Michael Martone (Iowa City: University of Iowa Press, 1988), 43.

2. Yi-Fu Tuan, *Space and Place: The Perspective of Experience* (Minneapolis: University of Minnesota Press, 1971), 149.

3. Ibid.

4. Michael Martone, "The Flatness," A *Place of Sense*, 32–33.

5. Erdrich, "A Writer's Sense of Place," 39.

6. Ibid.

7. David Mamet, *Glengarry Glen Ross* (New York: Grove, 1992), 14–15.

8. Tennessee Williams, A *Streetcar Named Desire* (New York: Signet, 1964), 83–84.

9. Suzan-Lori Parks, *The America Play and Other Works*, (New York: Theatre Communications Group, 1995), 174.

10. Una Chaudhuri, *Staging Place: The Geography of Modern Drama* (Ann Arbor: University of Michigan Press, 1995), 8.

11. Ibid., 10.

12. Ibid., 56.

13. Ibid., xiii.

14. Ibid., 138.

15. Greg Romero, *Cowboy River* (play in progress, University of Texas at Austin, 2004).

16. Carson Kreitzer, *Flesh and the Desert* (play in progress, University of Texas at Austin, 2004).

17. For information about Laban's system of Effort/Shape, see Rudolf Laban and Lisa Ullman, *Mastery of Movement* (London: Northcote House Educational, 1988).

9

CHAPTER

Architectural Space

IN THE PREVIOUS CHAPTERS WE HAVE EXPLORED A VARIETY OF SPACES that exist inside and outside of ourselves. As adults we find child space primarily in the domain of memory. Psychophysical space exists in both mind and body. Dream space resides in the unconscious. Mythic and sacred space is experienced on a spiritual plane. The multiple worlds of dimensional space can be accessed by crossing the thresholds that separate one metaphysical dimension from another. Interpersonal space is created between and among other people. Geographical space is found in a deeply personal sense of location. Each of these concepts of space can be thought of as a metaphorical landscape that exists as an internal state of being or awareness. Architectural space is slightly different in that it is always made manifest in external structures, such as buildings or bridges, or in a deliberate arrangement of natural elements, such as parks or gardens, or in comprehensive planned developments such as housing projects, cities, and towns. In architectural space, form and function are inseparable; spaces are conceived and created according to some kind of plan to accommodate specific activities.

Humans are not the only builders of architectural space. Birds build nests from bits of twigs, grasses, flowers, paper, gum wrappers, dryer lint, and sometimes the down from their own breasts for the sole purpose of sheltering their eggs and raising their offspring. Bees, ants, and termites construct communities with distinct areas for feeding, mating, egg laying, resting, and defending themselves against invaders. Sea turtles dig deep incubators in the sand to warm and protect their clutches of eggs. Caterpillars spin the cocoons of their miraculous transformations into butterflies. These architects of nature follow the blueprints of instinct, refined over generations of trial and error in a process of natural selection. If their structures are not sound, the species does not survive. Human beings, on the other hand, build structures for all kinds of reasons other than shelter and survival: for commerce, recreation, education, entertainment, and so on. Architectural space must constantly mediate between form and function, aesthetics and activity.

Principles of architectural theory and design have much in common with the craft of playwriting and the performance of theatre. In fact we often refer to a play's architecture as another term for its structure. Just as most buildings are made up of common elements such as doors, windows, ceilings, floors, walls, and staircases, most plays contain common elements of character, theme, plot, spectacle, and multiple forms of visual, verbal, and kinesthetic language. What is important in architecture, as in dramatic structure, is how these elements work together as a unified whole. Our buildings shape our thoughts and control our actions, just as we create structures that reflect the values and priorities of our culture.

I have long been fascinated by the spatial relationships that exist between theatre architecture and the plays produced within them. The great amphitheatres of the ancient Greeks built into the sides of mountains reflect a culture, a literature, and a sacred tradition where gods and humans walked, talked, had sexual relations, fought, and died together. The pageant wagons of the medieval mystery plays clearly designated a heaven above and a hell below and reflected a social hierarchy where classes were sharply differentiated and matters of faith were dominated by liturgy. Baroque opera houses and Restoration playhouses, with their wide loges and prominent boxes, placed primary emphasis on the audience rather than the performers. The plays and operas of this period depicted the graces and disgraces of a social and intellectual elite. In most theatrical spaces today, a lobby or central gathering place provides the social space for the audience, but the theatre itself is designed to disappear during the performance and to focus the audience's attention on the playing space. Theatrical space has always mirrored the form and content of performance, be it a ritual enacted in a circle of beaten earth by firelight, a court entertainment at the Palace of Versailles, or performance art in an abandoned factory.

Playwrights and architects build structures to contain events. For the playwright, the event is a live performance shared with an audience. For the architect, it is usually a building or series of structures with a specific purpose. Plays are usually conceived, designed, and produced as collaborative activities, not unlike the construction of a building. We often speak of a play as a blueprint for a production. The playwright, like the architect, is dependent on the excellence of others to achieve the fullness of his or her vision. No matter how beautiful the blueprint or how eloquent the script, unless these plans are well served by those who will actually build the house or create the performance, the effort is doomed to failure.

LIVING STRUCTURE

At the heart of architectural space is always structure. Structure may refer to a tangible entity—a building, bridge, framework, or other object—that has been put together from many different parts. In a more general sense, structure also refers to the system or organization of interrelated parts functioning as an orderly whole. In A *Pattern Language*, architect Christopher Alexander refers to structure as a simple picture that allows one to grasp an overall design as a whole. Alexander suggests that a structure should have as few elements as possible to allow one to clearly see the relationships that exist between the parts and to understand the pattern of those relationships. "What gives a building or a town meaning is the fabric of the relationships between elements and events." [1]

In his four-volume masterwork, *The Nature of Order: An Essay on the Art of Building and the Nature of the Universe*, Alexander presents a new theory of architecture based on deeply humanitarian concepts of wholeness and connection that have wide applicability beyond the fields of architecture and design. At the core of Alexander's work is an inquiry as to how humans inhabit space and how space inhibits or promotes a "feeling of life." Alexander presents a holistic notion of the universe as a series of interconnected centers in which everything, organic and inorganic, has a degree of life that is perceived through feelings. He conceives of a world in which "the air we breathe, the stones, the concrete our city streets are made of—all have a degree of life in them, or not . . . Life is a quality of space itself." [2]

Even in nature some spaces brim with vitality, energy, and a feeling of forward motion while others seem static, claustrophobic, and contained. A wave rolling in an elegant arc onto a moonlit beach feels alive; it has motion, shape, rhythm, momentum, and a kind of joy as a spray of water is released into the air. The same beach at low tide feels less alive, even though it may actually contain the same amount of biological particulate matter. The quality of deep life that is found in nature is also made manifest in all great art. Alexander calls this force "living structure." He believes that if something is structurally "real," all of its parts work together in harmony to accomplish the intention of its being. The life we feel in things comes from the fact that they are genuine, that they are deeply and truly themselves.

The term *living structure* resonates with those of us who work in the performing arts. The living structure of theatre takes place in real time and real space in the emotional and kinesthetic bonds that happen in performance. In speeches and keynote addresses, Ben Cameron, Executive Director of Theatre Communications Group, has frequently referred to the "deep listening" that takes place during a performance, a kind of intimacy that develops between spectator and performer that comes as a direct result of the fact that both are in the same physical place at the same time. On some level there is a mutual recognition of a shared humanity. This is never duplicated in quite the same way in the experience of seeing a film or television program.

PATTERNS

Christopher Alexander points to the importance of recurring patterns in the elements and events that determine the basis of architectural design. "Indeed, each building or town is ultimately made out of these patterns in the space, and out of nothing else: they are the atoms and the molecules from which a building or a town is made."[3] In Alexander's lexicon, the basic elements found in architecture, design, and even nature are called "centers." To Alexander, a center is an organized zone of space that has an internal coherence and a relationship to its context. A center is part of a larger whole and may indeed be a whole itself, composed of smaller centers. The geometrical shapes of triangles, squares, and circles in a design for a painted ceramic tile may individually be centers, as would be the white areas of negative space between them. The tile itself may be considered a center in the larger pattern of the entire floor. The floor may be considered a center in the overall design of the room, and the room functions as a center in the plan of the whole house. In this way it is possible to glimpse the overall structure of a house and a room and a floor and a tile and a circle, square, and triangle as individual yet interconnected.

The same principles of patterns of relationships between elements and events hold true in playwriting. If we think of a character as an agent of action, we see that character is a component of plot. If we consider theme to be all of the questions asked by the play, and not a single meaning or message, we realize that theme is intimately connected to both character and plot. In plays, as in architecture, each center is made up of many other centers.

Playwright and master teacher Sherry Kramer refers to the "systems" of a play in much the same way as Alexander talks about centers. Every play has many systems working concurrently and building cumulatively over time. A character may become a system as he or she develops and changes. An image, recurring phrase, or repeated behavior becomes a system when the context shifts its meaning in some way. The importance of systems is how they accrue meaning over the course of the play. For example, in my own play *Step on a Crack*, I used repeated knock-knock jokes as a system throughout the play. The play deals with a young girl's difficulty in accepting her new stepmother. In the beginning of the play, knock-knock jokes are used as a kind of code between Ellie and her father, Max. When the stepmother, Lucille, attempts to join in the fun and answers a knock-knock joke, Ellie abruptly terminates the game and excludes her. At the end of the play, when Ellie has come a bit closer to accepting Lucille, she initiates the following exchange:

ELLIE

Uhhhh, Lucille, knock, knock . . .

LUCILLE

Who's there?

ELLIE

Sticker.

LUCILLE

Sticker who?

ELLIE

Sticker-ound for a while, okay?[4]

It is the interaction of pattern and change that makes a system a system. Patterns also form the basis of choreography, in the movement of dancers, their repeated gestures, spatial arrangements, and the rhythm, tempo, and pace of their energies. If there is no relationship between component parts, if movement, gestures, and spatial arrangements are all totally random, there is no cohesion, and the piece does not work. When a play or a scene does not work, the spectator, and sometimes the performers, becomes confused and says, "I didn't get it." Sometimes this means "I didn't understand it." But more frequently, it means that no emotional connection has been made.

Emotional connection is often the result of a system that has functioned effectively: something has been set up early in the piece and pays off at its conclusion. The spectators share a moment of illumination, insight, or emotion in a mutual exchange of energy.

In his theory of architecture, Christopher Alexander believes that this felt connection to space is at the very heart of effective design and, indeed, effective living. In art, as in architecture, when all systems are fully developed and all centers are working together to support and strengthen one another, the process we call function is truly in harmony with the moving systems of life. "The deepest living structure is reflective of the deepest self in all of us, and of each of us as individuals, most profoundly."[5]

FUNDAMENTAL PROPERTIES

In *The Phenomenon of Life*, the first book of *The Nature of Order*, Alexander identifies fifteen fundamental properties of good design, which are as applicable to playwriting as they are to architecture. Alexander identifies these as structural features that tend to be present in examples of nature, art, and architecture that have a high degree of life. In the interest of brevity and clarity, I have selected eight properties that seem to have the most direct relevance to playwriting.

Strong Centers

A center is an element of wholeness. Centers are everywhere in art and in nature. Strong and mutually supportive centers are as essential to natural processes as they are to good design and to architectural order. On a most elemental level, the nucleus is the central organizing force of atoms, molecules, nerve cells of the central nervous system, and galaxies in outer space. Houses or office buildings without strong centers have no central gathering places where families or business associates can come together for mutual support and exchange.[6]

In a play, strong centers are those focal points that clarify what the play is truly about. In some cases this might mean a well-developed protagonist or a thematic issue that poses the central question of the play or a galvanic event that triggers or culminates the forward momentum of the action. Plays without strong centers seem to go off in many directions without a central organizing concept. This need not be a linear sequential story, but within every play there must be some gravitational force that keeps the diverse elements of the play in orbit around each other. Ask yourself, "If my play were a solar system, what part of it would be the sun?"

Boundaries

Living centers are nearly always formed and strengthened by the presence of clearly defined boundaries. In nature this can be seen in the walls of cellular structures, the corona of the Sun, and the banks of tidal pools. In design, borders help to define the central focus of an interior space. The fence that surrounds and contains a garden is as important as the flowers and plants within its boundaries.

In plays, boundaries exist on personal, psychological, and even spiritual levels for the characters and the themes you are exploring. Ask yourself, "Do the boundaries in my play hold characters, ideas, and images together or keep them apart? What happens when these boundaries are crossed?"

Alternating Repetition

One of the ways centers help each other most effectively is repetition. This is not simple repetition of the same thing over and over again, but repetition with variation and alternating patterns.[7] Most things in nature are made from some form of repetition: cellular division, crystal formation, the vein pattern of leaves and ferns. "It is the subtle variation that is satisfying and life-giving."[8] Too much repetition without variation, however, operates as the law of diminishing returns and becomes simply boring, as can be seen in the difference between an architectural arcade of ascending arches and a row of windows in a concrete blockhouse.

In playwriting, the repetition of words, phrases, and even actions and events with subtle variations builds momentum and emotional velocity. The repeated entrances of the Boy in *Waiting for Godot* are intriguing at first and ultimately inevitable; we know from the moment we see him that Godot is *not* coming. As the play ends, we imagine that the following day will simply repeat the patterns of waiting for a Godot who will never come. Ask yourself, "*Why* am I using repetition? Why *am* I using repetition? Why am I *using* repetition? "Why am I using *repetition*?"

Positive Space and Negative Space

"A work of art has more or less life to the extent that *every* single one of its component parts and spaces is whole, well-shaped, and positive."[9] The elimination of extraneous or unnecessary elements and the creation of a background of negative or neutral space give meaning to the essential centers that remain. In the crazed pattern of a porcelain glaze or the crackle of tiny lines of a raku pot, both the cracks and the spaces they create form the design. In a building, the negative space of open areas between rooms is as important as the rooms themselves.

In a play, negative space occurs in pauses, in silence, and in the beats between beats. In the dialogue of Harold Pinter, pauses are scored as stage directions. Suzan-Lori Parks makes great use of negative space in the spacing of dialogue and stage directions on the page. She clearly indicates the rhythm of a scene with multiple pauses indicated either as "(Rest)" or as empty space following a character's name. Whole scenes are built with these open spaces, left provocatively empty.

The winnowing away of nonessential elements is one of the most difficult and rewarding parts of a playwright's job. All of us have felt a relief tinged with sadness when a favorite line or scene or character is cut to serve the greater good of the play as a whole. Although the pain is intense at the moment, once the scene or speech or character is gone, it is often like it never existed. Suddenly, the scene or speech has breath, and the life force of the play surges. Ask yourself, "How can I say the most in the fewest possible words?"

Contrast

"Many—perhaps all—natural systems obtain their organization and energy from the interaction of opposites."[10] On the most fundamental biological levels, the union of male and female cells results in the formation of a new being, positive and negative electrical charges produce energy, and both light and darkness are essential to the process of photosynthesis. All design depends on contrast in color, texture, shape, and line to create differentiation, vitality, and intensity. In a building, "contrast, instead of separating things, brings them together."[11]

Throughout this book we have stressed the importance of oppositional forces in generating the tensional relationships that create dramatic action. Internal contrast in attitudes and attributes, motivations and desires creates depth of character, just as ethical complexity comes in the exploration of ideas and moral standards that are in conflict. All action is based in some form of conflict, and conflict is the direct result of contrast and oppositional forces. Ask yourself, "What are the tensional forces at work in all aspects of the play?"

Gradients

When one thing changes slowly and becomes another thing, all of the points of transformation along the way are gradients. "Gradients will follow as the natural response to any changing circumstance in space, as centers become adapted correctly to the changes which move across space."[12] The spectrum of a rainbow becomes a gradient of color as purple changes to blue to red to orange to yellow to green. In the design of Gothic cathedrals, gradients in the height and dimension of arched windows give the building a vaulted, uplifting feeling of rising to the heavens.

Concepts of change and transformation are vital to dramatic structure. There must be change of some kind from the beginning of the play or performance piece to the end. The most obvious forms of change take place in character and plot. A character dies or is born or leaves or stays or is blamed or forgiven. More subtle forms of change may take place in ideas or images. Ionesco's absurdist play *The Chairs*, begins with an empty stage; throughout the action of the play, individual chairs are added until the play ends with a stage filled with chairs. In some existential plays, the lack of change onstage underscores the impossibility of change for the characters. In *Waiting for Godot* and *No Exit*, change takes place in the audience as we slowly realize that Godot will never come and that exit is impossible. Ask yourself, "How does change happen in my play, and what causes change to happen?"

The Void

"In the most profound centers which have perfect wholeness, there is at the heart a void which is, like water, infinite in depth, surrounded by and contrasted with the clutter of the stuff all . . . around it."[13] Alexander points to the eye of a storm and the center of a vortex as the stillness that draws the energy of the center into itself and provides strength to the swirling energies that surround it. In many religious buildings, there is a central space that is intentionally left empty. Silence is often at the heart of sacred space. "Even a barn, the most practical of buildings, has a great emptiness. . . . The emptiness is needed, in some form, by every center, large or small."[14]

The heart of theatrical space is usually a void. The ancient Greek amphitheatres and the Elizabethan wooden O have great empty spaces at their centers. Contemporary theatre spaces such as arena and thrust stages often feature an expanse of empty space to be filled by actors and minimal set pieces. Even in proscenium theatres, the very center of the frame is often intentionally left open.

Even more important to playwrights is the sense of the void that brings magnitude to character and depth to thought. At the center of the swirling pretensions and fantasies of Blanche DuBois in *A Streetcar Named Desire* is an unfathomable emptiness. At the core of the quiet of Hanna Jelkes in *The Night of the Iguana* is a deep despair. Virtually all of the characters of Beckett face an existential void as deep as any black hole in space. The bravado and humor in Paula Vogel's *Baltimore Waltz* is the outward face of deep grief. A playwright's willingness and ability to embrace the void, even in comedy, is much more than an issue of craft; it is a matter of courage. Ask yourself, "At the center of myself, what is the unnamed void that I have yet to face, and how can that place of darkness illuminate my work?"

Not-Separateness

The most important principle of all, according to Alexander, is that a structure has a sense of being connected to its surroundings and to the rest of the living world. Every system in nature is part of a larger system, from atoms to galaxies. In architecture, a building has living structure to the extent that it dwells in harmony with its surroundings.

In playwriting, this principle is made manifest in the relationship you have to your work. In the best of times in your writing life, the play seems to come from somewhere and pass through you on its way somewhere else. Characters, ideas, thoughts, and themes inhabit the room of your mind as you listen and try to give them shape and definition. Once they move onto the page, they have their own life. Paradoxically, the concept of not-separateness also suggests that your writing is *not* separate from you or from your experiences, your beliefs, your passions, or your fears. Indeed, this whole book has been about finding this sense of connectedness of body and mind and greater self-use in your work. But the self we are talking about is a deeper kind of self than we usually access on a daily basis. This notion of self transcends individual tastes or cultural differences and is not unlike Jung's concept of collective unconscious. The buildings, artifacts, and works of art that affect us most profoundly are those in which we recognize something that is both personal and universal at the same moment. This is also true in the process of creation. The connectedness we seek between ourselves and our writing is a kind of fusion where our individual selves are inextricably connected to the characters, images, themes, and thoughts of the play, where we speak through them as they speak through us, where we must disappear in order to find ourselves most fully. Ask yourself, "In the mirror of my work, what reflections allow me to glimpse a self that I have never seen before?"

Throughout this book, Jim and I have used a mind-body synthesis to suggest specific activities to help you access wholeness in your processes of creation. We have provided exercises to promote a state of quiet awareness and tranquility, leading to ease and economy of motion while, at the same time, energizing thought into action. In the following section, we will return to the Warm-Up for writers from Chapter 1 to give some easy, quick exercises you can do at your desk to ease tension and stress. We also provide a few exercises to help you use the principles of Alexander's theories of architecture to help you explore the living structure of your work.

MOVEMENT: WARM-UP FOR WRITERS II

The following exercises are not meant to fix anything; rather, they are offered as a way of preventing something injurious from happening to your body over time. These exercises are easy and appear fairly effortless, but greater effort does not mean better action. At some point your body will tell you where you hold stress, where your tensions reside, and what parts of your body are out of alignment. These exercises may help you relax that tension and ease that strain. The body is a vast interconnected system where tension in one area may manifest somewhere else and release can affect the body as a whole.

Exercise for **Neck Tension, Headache, and Eye Strain**

This is sometimes called "the claw." It can be done while sitting or standing.

Take a relaxed hand and place it on the back of the neck with the little finger edge under the occipital ridge.

Your fingers should be resting on the muscles on the opposite side of the cervical spine.

Grip hard with the fingers, exerting pressure on the muscles as you slightly lift with the entire hand.

Keep the squeeze on the neck and slowly turn your head from right to left.

Do this several times.

While keeping the pressure on the squeeze, nod the head up and down.

Repeat several times.

Return to moving the head from side to side, but this time allow the eyes to lead the movement.

Nod your head up and down, but be careful to avoid collapsing the neck.

You will discover how much more freely your head will move, especially on the side of the neck that has received the pressure from the fingers.

Repeat the entire process with the other hand.

Exercise for the Pelvis and Lower Back

This is best done when seated. Push away from your desk, as you will need some space in front of your chair.

Reach forward and grasp the right knee with both hands.

Open the elbows out as you lift the knee toward the chest, clearing the foot from the floor.

While holding on to the knee, allow the foot to reach the floor, making full contact with the bottom of the foot.

Establish a rocking motion as you pull the knee up toward the chest and rock forward to make contact with the floor.

Repeat several times; then change knees and repeat many times.

Include full breaths with each movement. Breathe in through the nose as you lift the knee toward the chest and exhale through the nose as you rock forward to touch the foot to the floor.

Avoid making this move effortful; set up an easy back-and-forth rocking, and afterward you will experience release in the lower back and an ability to sit upright with a lengthened spine.

Exercise for Pelvis, Arms, Hands, and Shoulders

From a seated position, place your hands on your thighs, palms down.

Slowly and lightly press your hands over your thighs and move down to the knees, then down the outsides of the legs to your ankles.

Allowing your torso to bend forward, follow the arms and be sure that your head and neck are free and that you allow your spine to lengthen.

Direct your thought to free the neck, lengthen the spine, and allow your shoulders to broaden.

Once your hands have passed over the ankles, move the right hand out in front of the right foot.

Flatten your hand on the floor and make several clockwise rotations and several counterclockwise rotations with your palm on the ground.

Repeat the process with the left hand.

Now, bring your torso back to an upright position, allowing the hands to return over the outside of the legs and onto the thighs.

Remember to include an awareness of breath.

Inhale through the nose as you move forward.

Exhale as you rotate your hands on the floor.

Inhale as you return to upright.

Exhale while in the upright position.

Repeat this entire process several times.

Exercise for Torso, Head, Neck, and Eyes

Sit with your right hand on your left shoulder with both knees together and turned to the left. You are facing front.

Rotate the torso to the left several times.

Return the torso to the frontal position after each rotation.

Allow the head to turn with the torso.

After several repetitions, move the eyes first, then the head to the right as your torso moves to the left.

All return to full front.

Repeat several times.

Do the entire process with your left hand on your right shoulder and both knees together, turned to the right.

Hold the torso to the left, lift your face toward the ceiling and gaze down at the floor.

Repeat several times before turning the torso to the right and repeating the head and eye movements.

Exercise for Fingers and Wrists

Sit with your hands on any surface, such as the top of your desk.

Without placing any pressure on the wrist or fingers, try the following:

Place the hand flat on the surface.

Lift the fingers all at once, then individually.

Now, spread the fingers wide apart then move them back together.

Repeat several times with each hand.

Lift the hand while keeping the wrist in contact with the surface.

Lift the wrist while keeping the fingers in contact with the surface.

With the palm of the hand facing the surface, rotate the hand so

the back of the hand is on the surface.

Flip back and forth several times.

Turn the hand now to the little finger edge and rotate it over to the
thumb edge.

Rotate back and forth several times.

Lift the wrist until the hand is up on the fingertips.

Walk the fingers back and forth and from side to side.

Keeping a loose hand, lift the wrist and push the hand forward

onto the fingers and then to the back of the hand.

Rotate the hand, allowing the wrist to be the fulcrum.

Rotate in both directions.

ARCHITECTURAL SPACE EXERCISES

Although we spend most of our lives in architectural space, we seldom take
the time to really notice the structure of a particular space or to analyze how
it affects us in our attitudes and activities. All too often we simply take our
surroundings for granted, and only if the space is particularly beautiful or if it
inhibits our activities in some way does it register on our consciousness. In
the following exercises you will be invited to explore architectural space and
to use your experiences as prompts for writing.

Observation and Analysis

For this activity you will need to find and go to two architectural spaces, one
that engenders a strong feeling of living structure and one that does not. Rely
entirely upon your intuition and the felt sense of the dynamics of each place.
If possible, try to find structures that are somewhat the same, yet different,
rather than structures that have no similarities at all. There is often a feeling
of life in traditional buildings and utilitarian spaces.[15] An empty barn filled
with freshly baled hay with shafts of sunlight slanting through the walls may
indeed feel more alive than a corrugated tin warehouse. Both are storage
structures, both serve similar functions, both are utterly without self-
conscious ornamentation, yet one feels more alive than the other.

For this exercise you might use two living rooms—one where the life of a
family inhabits every element and one where everything is color coordinated,

neatly arranged, and encased in plastic slipcovers; or two grocery stores—one a whole-foods co-op with wooden floors and bins overflowing with grains and baskets of vegetables and the other a chain superstore; or two parks—one where natural forms and objects invite play and relaxation and the other where supersized playground equipment dictates virtually all of the activity.

In each space, take a few minutes to explore and analyze your reactions.

Movement

How does your body feel in this space?

Which elements of the space inhibit your movement?

Which elements permit movement through the space?

How does this space affect your behavior or the behavior of those around you?

Do your feelings change in various parts of this space?

Sensory Perception

What do you see, hear, smell, taste, and feel?

What are the predominant colors and textures in the space?

What are the lines and shapes that make up the space?

What is the rhythm of the space (visual and auditory)?

Fundamental Properties

Make a list of the strong centers contained in this space.

What are the boundaries of this space?

Are there examples of alternating repetition in the space?

Can you identify uses of positive and negative space?

How many examples of contrast can you find in the space?

What are the gradients you observe visually and kinesthetically?

Is there a void in this space?

How are all of the centers and events of the space interconnected?

How does this space serve as a mirror of the self?

What is the degree of life that you feel in this space?

Gestalt the Space
Describe each space in the voice of the space.

Sketch the Space
Using a sketchpad and charcoal pencil, quickly sketch at least fifteen drawings of each space and its various elements.

Sketch only the lines of the space.

Sketch only the shapes of the space.

Sketch the ground plan of the space.

Sketch the interplay of light and shadow in the space.

Make a sketch that emphasizes positive space (taken up by specific objects or elements).

Make a sketch that emphasizes negative space (open space that is *not* taken up with an object or element).

Sketch the rhythm of the space.

Writing from the Space
Write a ten- to fifteen-minute play that builds upon all of the preceding explorations for each space.

How are the worlds of these two plays different?

How are they the same?

How does the living structure or lack thereof affect the stylistic choices you are making for each play?

Staging Space
With a group of fellow writers or actors, return to each space and perform your play in the space.

How does the space contain or resist the play?

How do audience members who know they are spectators respond to the space?

How do spectators who just happen to be in the space but who do *not* know that a play is in progress seem to respond?

A WORD OR TWO . . .

For the writer, wholeness means having the courage to look into the mirror of the self and to use what you find there as the foundation for creating strong, living centers in your work. To do this, you must be willing to cross boundaries and to pare away all but the essential elements in the positive space of your plays. You must trust the stillness of silence and tolerate ambiguity as you embrace the contrast of opposites. Only then will you find transformation in yourself and in your work. When you are able to face the void, you will be able to see the interconnectedness of all things.

NOTES

1. Christopher Alexander, *A Pattern Language: Towns, Buildings, and Constructions* (New York: Oxford University Press, 1977), 87.

2. Christopher Alexander, *The Nature of Order: An Essay on the Art of Building and the Nature of the Universe*, Book 1: *The Phenomenon of Life* (Berkeley, CA: Center for Environmental Structure, 2002), 60.

3. Alexander, *A Pattern Language*, 75.

4. Suzan Zeder, *Step on a Crack* (New Orleans: Anchorage, 1976), 57.

5. Alexander, *The Nature of Order*, 444.

6. Ibid., 151–57, 251–56.

7. Ibid., 165–72, 257–60.

8. Ibid., 257.

9. Ibid., 173.

10. Ibid., 272.

11. Ibid., 202.

12. Ibid., 206.

13. Ibid., 222.

14. Ibid., 224–25.

15. Ibid., 40.

10

CHAPTER

The Space of Fear

THIS WAS NOT A CHAPTER I INTENDED TO WRITE. IT CAME ABOUT QUITE by accident as the result of an experience I had with what I can only call a writer's block . . . on this very book. The first eight chapters were written in a great rush of energy and enthusiasm during a summer and fall research leave. In the peace and serenity of our Colorado writing retreat, Jim and I hammered out chapter after chapter—poring over books and notes, revisiting old workshop plans, starting each morning with movement, writing into the evening— and everything went smoothly . . . until November. With the end of the leave looming and the return to my teaching duties imminent, I was suddenly seized by an almost total paralysis. I stared at the computer screen and nothing seemed to come. I judged everything immediately after writing it. I tore up pages, took long walks in the forest, and circled through the labyrinth time and time again. Jim tried to help, but I discounted everything he said, thinking he was just trying to make me feel better. Worse still, I began to judge everything that we had done thus far as worthless. The tone was wrong, the essays were too long, there was too little movement, too many exercises. Who ever heard of combining writing and movement and drawing and God knows what else? I suddenly realized that at the root of this turmoil was my fear that time for the leave was almost up and that the book would *not* be finished by the deadline that I had set for myself.

The cacophony of my own negativity virtually shut me down until I returned to the university for a few days to see a production of a play I had written several years before. The trip reminded me that at heart I am, and always will be, a playwright and that every playwright who has ever lived has had similar moments of self-doubt. Seeing my students again helped me remember that they too had faced crises of confidence and survived them. The time away from the daily demands of the book and the intervention of a gifted therapist helped turn things around. She helped me realize that I had created a space of fear and lost myself within it. The only way to escape was to write my way out word by word. I came back to the woods with a set of promises that I taped to the wall next to my desk:

1. I *forbid* myself to finish the book . . . remove the goal that has become the obstacle.
2. I will greet every writing day by simply "being" and see what happens.
3. I recognize that worry and regret come from my attempts to control time.
4. I will believe that I have all the time I need.
5. I will face the space of fear.

The space of fear is made of mirrors and filled with smoke. It is as much a space of creation as any we have explored in this book. Whether we acknowledge it or not, it is a space with which we are very familiar, though it goes by many other names: the space of too much to do, the space of endless research, the space of running out of time, the space of competition, the space of judgment. For some of us this space is a very busy place, filled with appointments, commitments, committees, people who *really* need us, telephone calls to make, and emails to answer. It is a place of doing, not being, a place where we run so fast that we never quite get around to the writing that really matters to us because we never quite have the time for that.

For others, the space of fear is a quiet place, filled with familiar habits. It is a comfortable cocoon spun from what we have been told we do well. In this space we write the same play over and over again: different characters, different settings, different plots, but the same play.

The experience of fear may be a passing flash of panic or a constant state of dread. It can be merely uncomfortable or truly traumatic, but for almost everyone, a journey through the space of fear is an inevitable part of the business of making art, just as it is an inevitable part of living.

In the space of fear it is never now. The present is eclipsed as the past and future pull us in opposite directions. In the past we remember pain or sorrow or suffering so sharp that it seems to be happening now. We hear old tapes of failures real or imagined. We rehearse regrets. What we could have done becomes what we should have done, and if we'd only done that, instead of what we did, we wouldn't be doing what we're doing now! We spin and spin in an orbit of time gone by and catapult into a future in which we have already made all the mistakes we have yet to make. We leap over the act of creation and jump into judgment of the finished product. The effort required to straddle both past and future is exhausting. It takes all the strength we have just to stay frozen in two time zones that do not exist.

The space of fear is filled with voices. We have heard these voices so often we think they are our own, but they're not! One is the voice of an eighth-grade teacher who confused writing and spelling and made you believe that you couldn't do either one. Another is the voice of the theatre critic who found it more facile to take a potshot than to give praise. Yet another is the voice of your mother, who loved everything you ever wrote; another is the voice of your lover, who didn't. There are also the voices of friends, who give you good intentions instead of feedback, and the voice of the teacher, who in both praise and criticism inadvertently made you afraid to take a risk. The voices blend into a sound so loud that it seems like silence.

The space of fear is filled with the good work of others and the judgments that you make about how your own plays fall short or how much better they are than those of your colleagues. Krishnamurti, a spiritual teacher from India, points out, "When you compare yourself with another, ideologically, psychologically, or even physically, there is the striving to become that; and there is the fear that you may not. . . . Where there is comparison there must be fear."[1]

The space of fear is filled with darkness and light. In the dark, we find ourselves lost in the play that started with so much promise. The character that was so witty and wise at first is now tiresome and trite. Plots, spun first in filaments of possibility, keep unraveling. When we turn on the light of our self-criticism, it is a halogen bulb of merciless intensity that makes every flaw, every imperfection, every mistake in our work so painfully visible that all we can see is what is wrong.

The space of fear is filled not with our failures, but with our most perfect play behind a wall of glass bricks, visible but unreachable. We realize that the play will never be all that it could be, or all that it *should* or might be if only we were just a teensy bit more talented! The possible play will always be better than the finished product. The idea incarnate holds limitless potential; with each word, it becomes more of what it is and less of what it might become.

On some level we all know that this fear is of our making. Lots of well-meaning folks will try to tell us to buck up, that what we fear isn't real, that we are being too hard on ourselves, but to be told that our fear is groundless denies the ground upon which we stand. To be told to just get over it diminishes the height of the wall.

GOOD FEAR, BAD FEAR

As we enter the space of fear, it is helpful to try to determine what kind of fear we are facing. Physical fear enables us to accomplish what we never thought we could do. Physiologically, the fight-or-flight mechanism heightens awareness and gives that shot of adrenaline necessary for the antelope to outrun the lion. In *The Gift of Fear*, Gavin De Becker posits the notion that fear is actually our strongest ally in times of real danger; it sends us the messages we should listen to and gives us the information we need to save our own lives. "Real fear is a signal intended to be very brief, a mere servant of intuition. . . . It is not an emotion like sadness or happiness that might last a long while. It is not a state, like anxiety. True fear is a survival signal that sounds only in the presence of danger, yet unwarranted fear has assumed a power over us that it holds over no other creature on earth."[2]

Psychological fear is something quite different from biological fear. It is a form of self-protection that makes us afraid of loss, disease, death, failure, falling short of expectations, and so on, before anything frightening really happens. This fear manufactures its own repercussions as we speculate, "What if?" As we spin scenarios of disaster, we are actually creating that which we fear the most. Throughout his teachings, Krishnamurti states that fear exists in thought and in word. The word is not the fact of fear, but the word engenders fear; unconsciously the whole structure is verbal.[3] We are so caught up in words and feelings that we become immobilized. We fear the dark because there *might* be something dangerous lurking. When we focus on the thing itself, there is often something we can *do*! If we fear the dark, we can turn on a light. If we fear the unknown, we can get to know it!

Every time you begin a new play, you enter unknown territory. No matter how successful your last play was or what kind of praise it garnered, every time you start, you start over. It is a cruel fact of our profession that tremendous success often sets you up for tremendous failure. Marsha Norman is said to have suggested that after winning the Pulitzer prize, a playwright should hire a ghostwriter to write his or her next play because it is doomed to fail.

Responses to Fear

When faced with fear, many people either deny that it exists or attempt to hide from it by repeating familiar patterns that seem to provide security. Neither of these strategies is particularly effective. Krishnamurti states, "So there is either repression or escape; and in trying to get rid of it, there is conflict which only increases the fear."[4] One of fear's strongest allies is denial, but it is crucial to recognize the difference between denial and defiance. Denial is when you refuse to recognize the presence of fear. To say that you are not afraid when you have every good reason to be is not an indication of courage; it just shows that you are not paying attention or you are lying to yourself. The effort of denial is exactly what feeds fear and allows it to grow unchecked. This is why fear often results in paralysis; you are simply too exhausted to do anything else. Defiance, on the other hand, is an active state. It demands that you recognize the adversary, understand the consequences, and choose to live your life as if the fear did not exist. To some, this might appear to be denial, but it is just the opposite. The ultimate engagement of fear is to deny its power in defiance!

In his book *The Craft of the Warrior*, Robert Spencer suggests that fearlessness begins with opening all of the senses and developing the ability to look at the world and into the self without deception. "Experiencing in such a direct fashion, without creating deceptions designed to shield you...is an act of warriorship and an act of fearlessness."[5] Both Spencer and Krishnamurti agree that the only way to deal with fear is to willingly and openly face it, to observe it without trying to escape it or analyze it or even accept it. "Fear ceases only when there is direct contact. When I have no escapes at any level, I can look at the fact. . . . To die means that you have to die every day, not just twenty years from now."[6] The first step in dealing with fear, then, is to recognize its presence, to call it by name, to draw its shape and dimension, to recognize the sound of its voice. To touch the face of fear is to get close enough to spit in its eye.

Learning from Fear

Krishnamurti takes the idea of recognizing fear one step further. It is not enough to simply face the fear and name it; he encourages us to learn from the fear by watching it without words. This is a tall order for writers, who use words as the primary currency of their thought and expression. Part of watching and attending to fear has to do with changing the image of that fear and being able to say, "I have no image of you. I am not afraid of you, because I have broken that image."[7]

Learning from fear is a matter not only of shattering old images and moving beyond fear but also of learning how to move with it, through it, and to use the power of its energy as a positive force for change. The space of fear is a hostile territory, but it is also the place where we are most ourselves, naked and vulnerable. It calls from us the courage needed to do something extraordinary—survive.

Survival Strategies

Fear, particularly the fear of failure that drives so many playwrights, dwells in worry about the future and in regret over the past. Both activities are equally counterproductive because neither has anything to do with the present. You find yourself up against a deadline and totally blocked. You say to yourself, "If only I had started working on this play months ago! Why did I waste so much time in research? Now I'll never be finished in time." But worrying is like trying to mold clay while it is still in the ground, and regret is like sculpting snow after it has melted. Focus on what is happening *now*, at this minute in the scene you are trying to write, the plot problem you are trying to solve, the character who is refusing to talk to you. Never mind, for the moment, whether the choice you are making is the right one; just make it! See what happens! In another moment there will be the possibility of making another choice. Writers are fortunate in that all we have to lift is words. If you are carving a two-hundred-pound block of marble, choices are very heavy!

In their book, *Art and Fear*, David Bayles and Ted Orland suggest that an artist's ability to embrace uncertainty is another survival strategy. "Making art is chancy—it doesn't mix well with predictability. Uncertainty is the essential, inevitable, and all pervasive companion to your desire to make art."[8] Spencer puts it another way: "Living fearlessly requires the warrior to be without doubt."[9] Uncertainty is not the same as doubt. Uncertainty opens the door to discovery, while doubt prevents you from crossing the threshold. When you are wandering through the space of fear, it is vital that you detach yourself from the outcomes that you cannot control. To do this, you need something that will sound very old-fashioned in these days of irony and cynicism. You need faith, a basic belief in the soundness of your vision, the competence of your collaborators, and the intelligence of your audience.

Trying to control what cannot be controlled and moving to the end of an experience before it is finished is called end gaining. It is not the same as fear, but it is closely related. It is, in fact, a defense against fear that, like denial, winds up feeding it. This doesn't mean that you should not care how something turns out but that you should keep your senses open, stay grounded in the present, and allow yourself to respond to change as it occurs. This is absolutely vital in the process of writing, as characters tend to take off in unexpected directions and events beget other events that may be, indeed should be, unforeseen and unplanned. If the play has any life at all, it has a life of its own.

There have been times in my writing life when my own characters scared me to death, as I had no idea whatsoever where they were going! They refused to obey the scenario I had so kindly set out for them. Invariably, they took me to a more interesting place than I had initially planned for them. When you are too attached to your initial outcome, you will accept only those ideas, images, and elements that support that outcome. You cut yourself off from everywhere else you could go and anything else that could happen. That anything else is the beating heart of your play. The energy from the space of fear can catapult you out of what you know and into what you can discover. Unless you fear something in your work, you are not aiming high enough.

There are times when a life in art seems to operate on a law of diminishing returns. The more you have accomplished, the more difficult it becomes to grow, to change, to give the public and the critics something other than what they have learned to expect from you. The most terrifying thing to an artist is not criticism but being ignored. Being invisible is far worse than being disliked. When I was a child my siblings and I used to torture my little sister by making her "disappear." We would pretend to look for her while she was standing right in front of us, shouting, "I am here! I am right *here!*"

In art, the simple act of acknowledgment is often more important than acclaim. Krishnamurti says that courage is not the opposite of fear; it is the ability to acknowledge fear and move through it. For an artist, it takes courage to stand and say, "I am *here!*"

It takes faith to believe that anyone cares!

EXERCISES FOR THE SPACE OF FEAR

1. Face your fear and name it.
2. To learn from fear, watch without words.
3. Stay in the present.
4. Embrace uncertainty.
5. Don't be attached to the outcomes that you cannot control.
6. Believe in the soundness of your vision, the competence of your collaborators, and the intelligence of your audience.
7. Allow fear to take you somewhere you have never been before.
8. Stand and say "I am here."

A WORD OR TWO . . .

Fear not!

NOTES

1. J. Krishnamurti, On Fear (San Francisco: HarperSanFrancisco, 1995), 2.

2. Gavin De Becker, The Gift of Fear (New York: Dell, 1998), 277.

3. Krishnamurti, On Fear, 40.

4. Ibid., 28.

5. Robert Spencer, The Craft of the Warrior (Berkeley, CA: North Atlantic, 1993), 126–27.

6. Krishnamurti, On Fear, 43.

7. Ibid.

8. David Bayles and Ted Orland, Art and Fear: Observations on the Perils (and Rewards) of Artmaking (Santa Cruz, CA: Image/Continuum, 1993), 21.

9. Spencer, The Craft of the Warrior, 127.

BIBLIOGRAPHY

Abrams, Jeremiah, ed. 1990. *Reclaiming the Inner Child*. Los Angeles: J. P. Tarcher.

Ackroyd, Peter. 1996. *Blake*. New York: Knopf.

Alexander, Christopher. 1977. *A Pattern Language: Towns, Buildings, and Constructions*. New York: Oxford University Press.

————. 2002. *The Nature of Order: An Essay on the Art of Building and the Nature of the Universe*. Book 1: *The Phenomenon of Life*. Berkeley, CA: Center for Environmental Structure.

Aristotle. 1969. *Poetics*. New York: Hill and Wang.

Aronson, Arnold. 1981. *The History and Theory of Environmental Sceneography*. Ann Arbor: University of Michigan Press.

Ashcraft, Norman, and Albert E. Scheflen. 1976. *People Space: The Making and Breaking of Human Boundaries*. New York: Anchor.

Bachelard, Gaston. 1994. *The Poetics of Space: The Classic Look at How We Experience Intimate Places*. Translated by Maria Jolas. Boston: Beacon.

Bayles, David, and Ted Orland. 1993. *Art and Fear: Observations on the Perils (and Rewards) of Artmaking*. Santa Cruz, CA: Image/Continuum.

Bray, Errol. 1995. *Playbuilding: A Guide for Group Creation of Plays with Young People*. Portsmouth, NH: Heinemann.

Breed, Donna, and David Kahn. 1995. *Scriptwork: A Director's Approach to New Play Dramaturgy*. Carbondale, IL: Southern Illinois University Press.

Brook, Peter. 1995. *The Empty Space*. New York: Touchstone.

Broudy, Harry. 1976. "Impression and Expression in Artistic Development." In *The Arts, Human Development, and Education*, edited by Eliot Eisner. Berkeley, CA: McCutcheon.

Burke, Kimberly. 2005. *Lacuna*. MFA thesis play, University of Texas at Austin, 2005.

Cameron, Jennifer. 2005. *The Little Mermaid*. MFA thesis play, University of Texas at Austin.

Campbell, Joseph. 1972. *Myths to Live By*. New York: Viking.

————. 1973. *The Hero with a Thousand Faces*. Princeton, NJ: Princeton University Press.

Castagno, Paul. 2001. *New Playwriting Strategies: A Language-Based Approach to Playwriting*. New York: Routledge.

Chatwin, Bruce. 1987. *The Songlines*. New York: Penguin.

Chaudhuri, Una. 1995. *Staging Place: The Geography of Modern Drama*. Ann Arbor: University of Michigan Press.

Cixous, Hélène. 1993. *Three Steps on the Ladder of Writing*. New York: Columbia University Press.

Cohen, Bonnie Bainbridge. 1994. *Sensing, Feeling and Action*. Northampton, MA: Contact Collaborations.

Cohen, Bonnie Bainbridge and Margret Mills. 1979. *Developmental Movement Therapy*. Amherst, MA: School for Body-Mind Centering.

Coles, Robert. 1990. *The Spiritual Life of Children*. Boston: Houghton Mifflin.

De Becker, Gavin. 1998. *The Gift of Fear*. New York: Dell.

Del Vecchio, Lucia. 2002. *theevolutionofwoman*. MFA thesis play, University of Texas at Austin.

Dickman, Matthew. 2004. *Repair*. MFA play in progess, University of Texas at Austin.

Dillard, Annie. 1989. *The Writing Life*. New York: Harper and Row.

Downs, William, and Lou Ann Wright. 1997. *Playwriting: From Formula to Form*. New York: Harcourt Brace.

Edwards, Betty. 1979. *Drawing on the Right Side of the Brain*. Los Angeles: J. P. Tarcher.

————. 1986. *Drawing on the Artist Within*. New York: Simon and Schuster.

Eliade, Mircea. 1959. *The Sacred and Profane: The Nature of Religion*. Translated by William R. Trask. New York: Harper.

Erdrich, Louise. 1988. "A Writer's Sense of Place." In *A Place of Sense*, edited by Michael Martone. Iowa City: University of Iowa Press.

Feldenkrais, Moshe. 1991. *Awareness Through Movement*. San Francisco: HarperSanFrancisco.

Flanagan, Owen. 2000. *Dreaming Souls: Sleep, Dreams, and the Evolution of the Conscious Mind*. New York: Oxford University Press.

Francis, Carlia. 1998. *Twilight's Ending*. MFA thesis play, University of Texas at Austin.

Friedman, Robert. 1996. *Playwright Power: A Concise How-to Book for the Dramatist*. New York: UP America.

Gardner, Howard. 1982. *Art, Mind, and Brain: A Cognitive Approach to Creativity*. New York: Basic.

———. 1991. *The Unschooled Mind*. New York: Basic.

———. 1993a. *Creating Minds: An Anatomy of Creativity as Seen Through the Lives of Freud, Einstein, Picasso, Stravinsky, Eliot, Graham, and Gandhi*. New York: Basic.

———. 1993b. *Frames of Mind: The Theory of Multiple Intelligences*. New York: Basic.

Garrison, Gary. 1999. *The Playwright's Survival Guide*. Portsmouth, NH: Heinemann.

Gogerty, Megan. 2003. *Love Jerry*. MFA thesis play, University of Texas at Austin.

Goldberg, Natalie. 1986. *Writing Down the Bones*. Boston: Shambhala.

———. 1993a. *Long Quiet Highway*. New York: Bantam.

———. 1993b. *Wild Mind*. New York: Bantam.

Grinder, John, and Richard Bandler. 1978. *Frogs into Princes*. Palo Alto, CA: Science and Behavior.

Hatcher, Jeffrey. 1996. *The Art and Craft of Playwriting*. Cincinnati: Story.

Houston, Jean. 1982. *The Possible Human: A Course in Enhancing Your Physical, Mental, and Creative Abilities*. Los Angeles: J. P. Tarcher.

Iizuka, Naomi. 1999. "What Myths May Come." *American Theatre Magazine* (September): 18.

John-Steiner, Vera. 2000. *Creative Collaborations*. New York: Oxford University Press.

Jung, Carl. 1964. *Man and His Symbols*. New York: Dell.

Kreitzer, Carson. 2004. *1:23*. MFA play in progress, University of Texas at Austin.

———. 2005. *Flesh and the Desert*. MFA play in progress, University of Texas at Austin.

Krishnamurti, J. 1995. *On Fear*. San Francisco: HarperSanFrancisco.

Laban, Rudolf, and Lisa Ullman. 1988. *Mastery of Movement*. London: Northcote House Educational.

Le Guin, Ursula K. 1980. *The Language of the Night: Essays on Fantasy and Science Fiction*. New York: Perigee.

Livingston Lowes, John. 1964. *The Road to Xanadu: A Study in the Ways of the Imagination*. Boston: Houghton Mifflin.

Lorenz, Konrad. 1963. *On Aggression*. Translated by Marjorie Kerr Wilson. New York: Harvest.

Mamet, David. 1992. *Glengarry Glen Ross*. New York: Grove.

Martone, Michael, ed. 1988. *A Place of Sense*. Iowa City: University of Iowa Press.

McAuley, Gay. 1999. *Space in Performance: Making Meaning in Theatre*. Ann Arbor: University of Michigan Press.

McCullers, Carson. 1951. *The Member of the Wedding*. New York: New Directions.

McLaughlin, Buzz. 1997. *The Playwright's Process: Learning the Craft from Today's Leading Dramatists*. New York: Back Stage.

Mehrabian and Ferris. 1967. "Inference of Attitudes from Non-verbal Communications in Two Channels." *The Journal of Counseling Psychology* 31: 248–52.

Merton, Thomas. 2000. "The Door That Ends All Doors." *Parabola: Myth, Tradition, and the Search for Meaning* 25: 96–98.

Metzger, Deena. 1993. *Writing for Your Life*. San Francisco: Harper.

Moon, Andrea. 2001. *Weight*. MFA thesis play, University of Texas at Austin.

Moore, Thomas. 2000. "Neither Here nor There: Psychotherapy and Religion Provide Tools for Deepening the Soul." *Parabola: Myth, Tradition, and the Search for Meaning* 25: 34–38.

Nakamura, Jeanne, and Mihaly Csikszentmihalyi. 2003. "Creativity in Later Life." In *Creativity and Development*, edited by R. Keith Sawyer. New York: Oxford University Press.

Nebadon, Michael. 2004. "Essential Balancing Through Unity in Motion." Speakers Platform. www.speaking.com/speakers/michaelcristiamnebadon.html.

Noble, Vicki. 1994. *Motherpeace: A Way to the Goddess Through Myth, Art, and Tarot*. San Francisco: HarperSanFrancisco.

Novak, Cynthia. 1990. *Sharing the Dance: Contact Improvisation and American Culture*. Madison: University of Wisconsin Press.

O'Connor, Joseph, and John Seymour. 2002. *Introducing Neuro-Linguistic Programming: Psychological Skills for Understanding and Influencing People*. London: Element.

Oddey, Allison. 1999. *Devising Theatre: A Practical and Theoretical Handbook*. New York: Routledge.

Packard, William. 1997. *The Art of the Playwright*. New York: Nation.

Park, Glen. 1989. *The Art of Changing: A New Approach to the Alexander Technique*. Bath, England: Ashgrove.

Parks, Suzan-Lori. 1995. *The America Play and Other Works*. New York: Theatre Communications Group.

Piaget, Jean, and Barbel Inhelder. 1956. *The Child's Conception of Space*. Translated by F. J. Langdon and J. L. Lunzer. New York: Humanities.

Pike, Frank, and Thomas Dunn. 1985. *The Playwright's Handbook*. New York: New American.

Rico, Gabriele. 1983. *Writing the Natural Way: Using Right Brain Techniques to Release Your Expressive Powers*. Los Angeles: J. P. Tarcher.

Romero, Greg. 2004. *Cowboy River*. MFA play in progress, University of Texas at Austin.

Schechner, Richard. 1994. *Environmental Theatre: An Expanded New Edition*. New York: Applause.

Shklovsky, Victor. 1965. "Art as Technique." In *Russian Formalist Criticism: Four Essays*, translated and with an introduction by Lee T. Lemon and Marion J. Reis. Lincoln: University of Nebraska Press.

Smiley, Sam. 1971. *Playwriting: The Structure of Action*. Englewood Cliffs, NJ: Prentice Hall.

Spencer, Robert. 1993. *The Craft of the Warrior*. Berkeley, CA: North Atlantic.

Sweet, Jeffrey. 1993. *The Dramatist's Toolkit: The Craft of the Working Playwright*. Portsmouth, NH: Heinemann.

———. 2001. *Solving Your Script: Tools and Techniques for the Playwright*. Portsmouth, NH: Heinemann.

Tuan, Yi-Fu. 1977. *Space and Place: The Perspective of Experience*. Minneapolis: University of Minnesota Press.

Williams, Tennessee. 1961. *The Night of the Iguana*. New York: New Directions.

———. 1964. *A Streetcar Named Desire*. New York: Signet.

Wright, Michael. 2001a. *Playwriting-in-Process: Thinking and Writing Theatrically*. Portsmouth, NH: Heinemann.

———. 2001b. *Playwriting Master Class: The Personality of Process and the Art of Rewriting*. Portsmouth, NH: Heinemann.

Zeder, Suzan. 1976. *Step on a Crack*. New Orleans: Anchorage.